And w

Great Is The Mystery Of Godliness:

God was manifested in
the flesh,

God was justified in the
Spirit, Seen by angels,

God preached among
the Gentiles,

God was believed on in
the world,

God was received up in
glory.

I Timothy 3:16

Do you know why Paul prayed for the church?

For this cause do I bow my knees unto the Father of our Lord Jesus Christ, of whom the whole family in heaven and earth is named. That He would grant you, according to the riches of His glory, to be strengthened with might by His Spirit in the inner man.

That Christ may dwell in your hearts by faith, and that by being rooted and grounded in love, you may be able to comprehend with all saints what is the breadth, and length, and depth, and height, and to fully know the love of Christ which passes knowledge, that you all might be filled with all the fulness of God.

Now unto Him that is able to do exceeding abundantly above all that we ask or think, according to that power that works in us, unto Him be glory in the church by Christ Jesus throughout all ages, world without end. Amen.

(Ephesians 3:14-21)

INTRODUCTION

Almost 2000 years ago the Apostle Paul wrote in his first epistle to Timothy that it was not **"Without controversy, great is the mystery of godliness..."** Well, without a doubt that statement is every bit as true today as it was the day Paul wrote it.

But how many believers today even know what this "mystery of godliness" is? Perhaps a quick look at the scripture Paul wrote will help to stir up our hunger for truth, understanding, and righteousness.

I Timothy 3:16 - And without controversy great is the mystery of godliness: God was manifest in the flesh, justified in the Spirit, seen of angels, preached unto the Gentiles, believed on in the world, received up into glory.

Clearly, this mystery pertains to the fact that "God was manifest in the flesh." But, if we want to glean all we can from these nuggets of golden truths that Paul has presented here, we must not lose focus that all that Paul is saying in this verse applies directly to God and those events which transpired due to His incarnation.

For not only is it true that "God was manifest in the flesh," for Paul continues to affirm these other truths that "[*God was also*] justified in the Spirit, [*God was*] seen of angels [*while manifested in the flesh, whereby He*], preached unto the Gentiles, [*God was*] believed on in the world, [*and God was*] received up into glory.

These truths here, as well as a thorough examination and scriptural reasoning of God's grace, are the purpose and heart of this book. For I wish to remind you that God's inspired Word encourages us to learn that "Wisdom is the principal thing. Therefore, get wisdom, and with all your getting, get understanding," (Proverbs 4:7)

But, what is this wisdom? Certainly, it is not the vain wisdom of this world, but that which quickens the spirit of man and makes him alive unto God.

I Corinthians 3:18 - Let no man deceive himself. If any man among you seems to be wise in this world, let him become a fool that he may be wise. 19 For the wisdom of this world is foolishness with God. For it is written, He takes the wise in their own craftiness. 20 And again, The Lord knows the thoughts of the wise, that they are vain.

Proverbs 9:10 - The fear of the LORD is the beginning of wisdom: and the knowledge of the holy is understanding.

If the beginning of wisdom is to fear the Lord, and the knowledge of the holy is understanding, then it might be said that the wisest thing anyone could set their heart to do is to seek both knowledge and understanding of God. For if there is a God, and be assured that there is, it becomes incumbent upon all of us to seek Him out and to discover how we might not only get along with Him, but please Him as well.

Knowledge is basically an awareness of facts of reality that pertain to the areas of who, what, when, and where; but understanding is having a firm mental grasp of knowledge to the point where it becomes a motivation and is exercised in the "why" and "how." It might be likened this way-

- Knowledge; the foundation for faith
- Understanding; the motive for faithfulness

Such is why the author of Hebrews stated that "faith is the substance of things hoped for, the evidence of things not seen," (Hebrews 11:1). Thus, it is our understanding of the things of God that enables us to be faithful and to be wholly converted into the overcomers Jesus Christ has called us to be. For consider these words of Peter –

II Peter 1:2 - Grace and peace be multiplied unto you through the knowledge of God, and of Jesus our Lord, 3 According as His divine power has given unto us all things that pertain unto life and godliness, through the knowledge of Him that has called us to glory and virtue: 4 Whereby are given unto us exceeding great and precious promises: that by these you might be partakers of the divine nature, having escaped the corruption that is in the world through lust.

And thus, through Peter's words above, we have introduced "grace" into our subject, and yes, it is amazing grace. But do people really understand God's gift of grace? This is critical for those professing Christianity. Because, if a believer fails to understand the purpose and workings of God's grace, then it is almost certain they will fall short of allowing it to accomplish all that God intended it to in their life.

Hebrews 4:1 - Let us therefore fear, lest a promise being given to us of entering into His rest, any of you should seem to come short of it. 2 For unto us was the gospel preached, as well as unto them: but the word preached did not profit them, not being mixed with faith[*fulness*] in them that heard it.

I know if you are reading this book, then surely you have heard already that it is "by grace you are saved." But, have you not also heard God's bemoaning cry that, "My people perish for lack of knowledge?"

Yet, be assured it is only by God's grace that we could even hope to have ears to hear the wisdom that the Spirit of God is desperately trying to speak to us. But still, we need to be listening and willing to respond to what the Holy Spirit is instructing us to *do* in order to escape the wrath that will come upon all those who choose to remain in their sins.

People tend to forget, or perhaps willfully ignore, that in Jesus speaking the admonitions to all the saints in the Seven Churches of Revelation, how He repeatedly stressed that all those wonderful promises He was making were only for the "overcomers," those who had "ears to hear what the Spirit says to the Churches."

Luke 21:36 - Watch you therefore and pray always that you may be accounted worthy to escape all these things that shall come to pass and to stand before the Son of man.

Contents

A brief note from the author...

Unfortunately, when scriptures are given only as references in books, most people rarely take the time to look them up. Sure, when a point being asserted crosses ones long-held opinion, some references might actually get checked out. But sometimes when beliefs are so ingrained, it is too easy to automatically judge the other's perspective as being wrong without ever bothering to examine the foundation of scripture provided whereupon the author's statement is being asserted. Others are either so confident or indifferent, they simply dismissively quit reading the article and casually move on to the next, or without any examination simply toss a book aside deeming it unworthy of their time. How far removed many believers are today from that noble Berean spirit that once searched the scriptures to see if the things being stated were true, (Acts 17:10, 11).

But those who do authenticate other writers' words with the scriptures referenced are well aware of the increased work and additional time that must be spent to responsibly prove the author's message. Therefore, it is my practice to include all scripture referenced in my writing; except for the one above placed there to make my point.

The labor of any Christian author should be like the labor of one who strings pearls to make a necklace to grace the neck of those who would choose to wear it. However, what I have written here can hardly be considered worthy to be the string whereby such priceless oracles are to be joined, seeing they were given to holy men of God. Men, who like the oyster, were often required to endure severe trials before the grace of God brought forth those glorious pearls of truth for the benefit of those who would receive them. Nevertheless, I assure you that this book is a labor of love and written in obedience to my Lord Jesus Christ.

Proverbs 3:19 - The LORD by wisdom has founded the earth; by understanding has He established the heavens. 20 By His knowledge the depths are broken up, and the clouds drop down the dew. 21 My son, let not them depart from thine eyes: keep sound wisdom and discretion: 22 So shall they be life unto thy soul, and grace to thy neck. 23 Then shall you walk in your way safely and your foot shall not stumble.

Therefore, it is my earnest recommendation that the reader make a commitment now before the Lord to read through all the verses in their entirety. After all, these pearls are His words and their inclusions are here for your benefit, so please take advantage of them.

The Necessity of Faith

Hebrew 11:6 - But without faith it is impossible to please Him: for he that comes to God must believe that He is, and that He is a rewarder of them that diligently seek Him.

I love the above verse, though I often quote it as an exhortation to others that "with faith *it is possible* to please Him." For God's greatest desire is to be sought after by His creatures that they might truly "know" Him. Thus, God has promised to reward men with understanding if they would but "diligently" seek Him. However, we are forewarned that it is only by picking up our crosses and following Him that we can succeed in truly following Him and have hope to answer His call to perfect holiness.

II Corinthians 7:1 - Having therefore these promises, dearly beloved, let us cleanse ourselves from all filthiness of the flesh and spirit, perfecting holiness in the fear of God.

For those who would by faith obey these mandates; to come to God, to please Him, and perfect holiness, Jesus said it would be given "to know **the mystery** of the kingdom of God."

Mark 4:9 - And He said unto them, He that has ears to hear, let him hear. 10 And when He was alone, they that were about Him with the twelve asked of Him the parable. 11 And He said unto them, "Unto you it is given to know the mystery of the kingdom of God: but unto them that are without, all these things are done in parable."

Those who truly desire "to know" this mystery, and not merely in a hollow doctrinal sense, will prove their heart's desire by determinedly seeking after it. For those who are given to complacency or slothfulness, the scriptures offer no hope that they will ever "find" what they will only half-heartedly "seek" after. One must actively "knock" as it were, spending their time and energy in dedicated prayers and studies if the door of understanding is to be permitted to be "opened" unto them.

Matthew 7:7 - Ask, and it shall be given you; seek, and you shall find; knock, and it shall be opened unto you: 8 For every one that asks receives; and he that seeks, finds; and to him that knocks, it shall be opened.

But guard your hearts and do not for a minute think your labors alone will be sufficient in their own merit or will provide you with intellectual strength enough to break through the partition of ignorance into divine understanding. For our Savior said it was only to His disciples that "It is given to know" these things. Therefore, you must not fail to recognize the importance of your coming under His discipline if you are truly aspiring to be His disciple.

Deuteronomy 4:29 - But if …you shall seek the LORD your God, then you shall find Him, if you seek Him with all your heart and with all your soul. 30 When you are in tribulation, and all these things are come upon you, even in the latter days, if you turn to the LORD your God, and will be obedient unto His voice; 31 (For the LORD your God is a merciful God;) He will not forsake you, neither destroy you, nor forget the covenant of your fathers which He swore unto them.

The greatest thing to "find" and "know" is God Himself. Even after Paul's great conversion and years of ministry, surpassing the other apostles in his labor, travels, ministries and revelations, his greatest motivation and desire was succinctly expressed in "That I might know Him."

Philippians 3:8 - Yea doubtless, and I count all things but loss for the excellency of the knowledge of Christ Jesus my Lord: for whom I have suffered the loss of all things, and do count them but dung, that I may win Christ, 9 And be found in Him, not having mine own righteousness, which is of the law, but that which is through the faith of Christ, the righteousness which is of God by faith: 10 That I may know Him, and the power of His resurrection, and the fellowship of His sufferings, being made conformable unto His death. 11 If by any means I might attain unto the resurrection of the dead. 12 Not as though I had already attained, or were already perfect: but I follow after, if that I may apprehend that for which also I am apprehended of Christ Jesus.

Before his conversion, the Apostle Paul was without a doubt one of the most educated men of his time apart from his mentor. For he had sat "at the feet of Gamaliel, and [*was*] taught according to the perfect manner of the law of the fathers," (Acts 22:3). However, with all his knowledge, Paul was still unable to really know God. After his encounter with Christ on the road to Damascus, Paul humbly withdrew himself for years to reexamine all he had previously and vigilantly held to be true.

How much more do we then need to humble ourselves and acknowledge the minuteness of our own scriptural knowledge and understanding if we too are to have any hope of being truly enlightened by God's Holy Spirit? For through his conversion the Apostle Paul discovered that nothing had been more blinding in his life or a greater hindrance to his truly serving God and receiving the truth, than that "light" he once proudly thought himself to have firmly possessed.

I Corinthians 8:2 - And if any man thinks that he knows anything, he knows nothing yet as he ought to know.

Likewise, such vain religious over-confidence continues to thrive unrestrainedly in Christendom today; making some professors of Christ the most arrogant and prideful men alive. Yet, more often than not, their knowledge often proves to be but empty theoretical strongholds that cause them to bunker down, throw up their shields, and spitefully take up arms against brothers of the faith. Often, it is with ridicule and closed-mindedness that they defend their long held and cherished historic positions and creeds.

When men are truly spiritually awakened, it is because they have been confronted with the reality that they needed to humble themselves, and always be willing to consider that what they have come to believe may not be correct or complete.

We must never forget that for success in seeking the truth, our efforts must be coupled with a sincere intention and readiness to yield ourselves wholly to the revelation of God's will. Otherwise, we have no right or grounds to expect to receive anything from God. For any man that loves his church, creed, ministry, job, retirement plan, or family more than he loves the Lord and the truth, then his own heart will remain to be his greatest hindrance.

James 1:5 - If any of you lack wisdom, let him ask of God, that gives to all men liberally, and withholds not; and it shall be given him. 6 But let him ask in faith, nothing wavering. For he that wavers is like a wave of the sea driven with the wind and tossed. 7 For let not that man think that he shall receive any thing of the Lord. 8 A double minded man is unstable in all his ways.

Willful sin in our lives creates an impassable obstacle to our coming to a liberating knowledge of the truth. It is only when "our hearts condemn us not" of loving sin or willfully hiding it in our hearts that we can possess true "confidence" toward God and have the faith and assurance that "whatsoever we ask, we receive of Him, because we keep His commandments and do those things that are pleasing in His sight," (I John 3:21, 22).

For even if we may not fully understand the will of God, our consciences nonetheless still have an inclination of right and wrong that works toward our honoring or dishonoring God. For though not all may have come to possess that strong faith that comes only through routine study of God's word and the application thereof, they still possess "a measure of faith" whereby they can seek and please God.

Romans 14:5 - One person esteems one day above another: another esteems every day alike. Let every man be fully persuaded in his own mind. 6 He that regards the day, regards it unto the Lord; and he that regards not the day, to the Lord he does not regard it. He that eats, eats to the Lord, for he gives God thanks; and he that eats not, to the Lord he eats not, and gives God thanks... 22 Do you have faith? Have it to yourself before God. Happy is the one that condemns not himself in that thing which he allows.

The Mystery of Godliness,
God was Manifested in the Flesh

I Tim. 3:16 - For without controversy, great is the mystery of godliness: God was manifested in the flesh, justified in the spirit, seen of angels, preached unto the Gentiles, believed on in the world, received up into glory.

The disclosure of divine truth concerning God's person to humanity has been a constant and incremental process, as is witnessed by the revelation of God's many names throughout time being revealed through the prophets. The following is but a short list taken from over 900 name variations assigned to God in scripture.

Adonai: *Lord, Master*

Elohim: *God*

El Elyon: *The Most High God*

El Olam: *The Everlasting God*

El Shaddai: *Lord God Almighty*

Jehovah Jireh: *The Lord Will Provide*

Jehovah Mekoddishkem: *The Lord Who Sanctifies You*

Jehovah Nissi: *The Lord My Banner*

Jehovah-Raah: *The Lord My Shepherd*

Jehovah Rapha: *The Lord That Heals*

Jehovah Sabaoth: *The Lord of Hosts*

Jehovah Shalom: *The Lord Is Peace*

Jehovah Shammah: *The Lord Is There*

Jehovah Tsidkenu: *The Lord Our Righteousness*

Qanna: *Jealous*

Yahweh: *Lord, Jehovah*

By these, we can see how throughout biblical history the revelation of God's person, as well as His truths, have been established one tidbit at a time; as holy men of old often prophesied in parts, "here a little" and then another time, perhaps even another prophet, "there a little." This method of enlightenment is in exact accordance with what the bible teaches us, for Paul tells us that even at our best, we all "know in part, and we prophesy in part," (I Corinthians 13:9).

Isaiah 28:9 - Whom shall He teach knowledge? and whom shall He make to understand doctrine? them that are weaned from the milk and drawn from the breasts. 10 For precept must be upon precept, precept upon precept; line upon line, line upon line; here a little, and there a little.

Friend, God is desirous to teach anyone who is old enough and willing to learn. Consequently, we must learn to quiet ourselves before the Lord and to wait on Him in His word, for it is often only there and then that the Holy Spirit will graciously begin to draw these parts together with His illuminating touch. For only He can cause each of these fragments of truth to lend their light so as to provide us with wonderful insight into what would otherwise remain veiled truths in scripture. For by this principle comes brilliant witness to the glory of God in Christ Jesus from our selected verse, which alone would otherwise be a puzzling piece of scripture.

I Tim. 3:16 - For without controversy, great is the mystery of godliness: God was manifested in the flesh, justified in the spirit, seen of angels, preached unto the Gentiles, believed on in the world, received up into glory.

Paul stresses in this verse that there exists an undeniably great mystery concerning godliness, an essential theme of the Gospel. For the Gospel is not just about Jesus dying on the cross to reconcile sinners unto God, it is much, much more than that.

Romans 5:8 - But God commended His love toward us, in that, while we were yet sinners, Christ died for us. 9 Much more then, being now justified by His blood, we shall be saved from wrath through Him. 10 For if, when we were enemies, we were reconciled to God by the death of His Son, much more, being reconciled, we shall be saved by His life.

Much more than just being reconciled to God, something many believers limit to a one-time event of "accepting Jesus" as their savior, Paul tells us "we shall be saved by His life." It is the life of Christ within men that saves them, not His death upon the cross; such is why Jesus came "confirming the covenant" of the resurrection, giving undisputable proof that what God has promised He can deliver.

Acts 1:2 - Until the day in which He was taken up, after that He through the Holy Ghost had given commandments unto the apostles whom He had chosen: 3 To whom also He shewed Himself alive after His passion by many infallible proofs, being seen of them forty days, and speaking of the things pertaining to the kingdom of God.

What I have said is not in any way to minimize Jesus' death; for it was absolutely necessary to appease the demands of God's righteous judgment, for "the wages of sin is death." Only by the death of Jesus Christ could anyone hope to be reconciled to

God, whereby God can enable us to be born again and quickened us by His word: that through the empowering of His Holy Spirit we might be brought "unto the measure of the stature of the fullness of Christ."

I Peter 1:21 - Who by Him do believe in God, that raised Him up from the dead, and gave Him glory; that your faith and hope might be in God. 22 Seeing you have purified your souls in obeying the truth through the Spirit unto unfeigned love of the brethren, see that you love one another with a pure heart fervently: 23 Being born again, not of corruptible seed, but of incorruptible, by the word of God, which lives and abides forever.

Ephesians 4:12 - For the perfecting of the saints, for the work of the ministry, for the edifying of the body of Christ: 13 Till we all come in the unity of the faith, and of the knowledge of the Son of God, unto a perfect man, unto the measure of the stature of the fullness of Christ: 14 That we henceforth be no more children, tossed to and fro, and carried about with every wind of doctrine, by the sleight of men, and cunning craftiness, whereby they lie in wait to deceive; 15 But speaking the truth in love, may grow up into

Him in all things, which is the head, even Christ.

God is not only holy, He alone is the wellspring of holiness and apart from Him there is no holiness. For that reason, God has commanded all His creatures to be holy; which can only be achieved by giving themselves wholly unto Him and His will in all things.

Leviticus 20:6 - And the soul that turns after such as have familiar spirits, and after wizards, to go a whoring after them, I will even set My face against that soul, and will cut him off from among his people. 7 Sanctify yourselves therefore and be you holy: for I am the LORD your God.

II Peter 1:13 - Wherefore gird up the loins of your mind, be sober, and hope to the end for the grace that is to be brought unto you at the revelation of Jesus Christ; 14 As obedient children, not fashioning yourselves according to the former lusts in your ignorance: 15 But as He which has called you is holy, so be you holy in all manner of conversation; 16 Because it is written, Be you holy; for I am holy.

Because holiness is inseparable from God, it is a fundamental aspect of godliness. As a matter of fact, the Greek word which was translated "godliness" here in 1st Timothy was translated "holiness" in the place it was first used in scripture. For holiness is Godlikeness.

Acts 3:12 - And when Peter saw it, he answered unto the people, You men of Israel, why marvel you at this? or why look you so earnestly on us, as though by our own power or *holiness* we had made this man to walk?

However, because "great is the mystery of godliness," mankind has been given to endless debates and illusions about the man Jesus Christ. It seems men cannot agree as to the purpose of His incarnation and the truth regarding His birth, death, and resurrection; and most importantly about His deity. Many of these debates and illusions were birthed out of a devilish attempt to conceal the fact that God was indeed "justified in the spirit [*and*] seen of the angels."

I Tim 3:16 - For without controversy, great is the mystery of godliness: **God was** manifested in the flesh, [*God was*] **justified in the spirit**, [*God was*] seen of angels, [*God had*] preached unto the Gentiles, [*God was*] believed on in the world, [*God was*] received up into glory.

The reason "God was... justified in the spirit" is in bold print and brackets is because many people often overlook it and fail to carry the subject matter through to its end; that "God was" in the person of Jesus Christ redeeming the world unto Himself.

II Corinthians 5:18 - And all things are of God, who has reconciled us to Himself by Jesus Christ, and has given to us the ministry of reconciliation; 19 To wit, that God was in Christ, reconciling the world unto Himself, not imputing their trespasses unto them; and has committed unto us the word of reconciliation.

Regardless of what Paul clearly wrote to Timothy and the church in Corinth, most Christians in our day and age fail to pause and focus on that fundamental part of the verse, that "God was... justified in the spirit." Over the years I have listened to various people discuss how God was "manifested in the flesh," and have listened to sermons using this verse being preached, only to hear preacher after preacher simply read over that part as if it were nothing more than some sort of King James jargon put there merely as some spiritual poetic-word-filler. But it's not. It's an extremely important confirmation to what has regrettably become a little known and taught part of the Christian faith. Sadly, I have only heard one other preacher expound on this "justified in the Spirit" aspect and he has passed on.

Part of the problem is the church has failed to be faithful stewards of the Gospel and to assertively preach the absolute deity of Jesus, not only as the prophesied "son of God" but as the scripture states, very God Himself manifested in the flesh. Partly because many ministers no longer believe it themselves. This can only be attributed to the clever working of the adversary; who does not mind men being religious. However, he hates it when they are lovers and proclaimers of this truth. For by it the devil with all the fallen powers of darkness were openly defeated by a man dying upon a cross.

Colossians 2:15 - And having spoiled principalities and powers, He made a show of them openly, triumphing over them in it.

II Corinthians 4:2 - But have renounced the hidden things of dishonesty, not walking in craftiness, nor handling the word of God deceitfully; but by manifestation of the truth commending ourselves to every man's conscience in the sight of God. 3 But if our gospel be hid, it is hid to them that are lost: 4 In whom the god of this world has blinded the minds of them which believe not, lest the light of the glorious gospel of Christ, who is the image of God, should shine unto them. 5 For we preach not ourselves, but Christ Jesus the Lord; and ourselves your servants for Jesus' sake. 6 For God, who commanded the light to shine out of darkness, has shined in our hearts, to give the light of the knowledge of the glory of God in the face of Jesus Christ.

Another Jesus, Another Gospel

II Corinthians 11:4 - For if he that comes preaches another Jesus, whom we have not preached, or if you receive another spirit, which you had not received, or another gospel, which you had not accepted, you might well bear with him [*who brought the gospel unto you*]. 5 For I suppose I was not a whit behind the very chiefest apostles.

Despite Paul's warning to the Corinth church that some would come "preaching **another Jesus**... [*and*] another gospel," most professing Christians are absolutely positive that they know who Jesus is. Therefore, they never even consider scripturally proving that their "Jesus" is the same one Paul preached about. However, in light of Paul's warning of "another Jesus," we would do well to examine our "Jesus" in the light of the "holy scriptures" while earnestly seeking the help of the Holy Spirit "to make you wise unto salvation through faith which is in Christ Jesus," (II Timothy 3:15).

Absolutely Jesus was and is called the "son of God." However, the word "son" was not intended to infer He would be God's descendant, or offspring such as we have offspring. For from the beginning the word was prophetic of the child's gender which God promised would be born. Back when Adam chose to sin in the garden, the Gospel went forth as God promised a deliverer would come; a "seed" would be raised up through the woman that would bruise the head of the serpent (the devil), and the serpent would "bruise HIS heel" (Genesis 3:15). Thus, it was prophesied a "man child" would be born.

Jesus Christ is that "seed" and "man child." A "son" that could only have been *of* God, for as foretold the child would be born of a virgin; making Him the prophetic "Son *of* God." Nevertheless, while this child's conception was entirely the predetermined plan and accomplishment *of* God, men would still call him a "son of man," (although no earthly man took part in His conception). For the phrase "son *of* man" is merely a Jewish or biblical expression that is intended to testify of one's humanity, as it is used by God and the angels toward Ezekiel ninety-three times. With Christ, "Son of man" testifies of His humanity; that He in fact was "born" a man.

Hebrews 2:14 – For as much then as the children are partakers of flesh and blood, He also Himself likewise took part of the same; that through death He might destroy him that had the power of death, that is, the devil; 15 And deliver them who through fear of death were all their lifetime subject to bondage. 16 For verily He took not on Him the nature of angels; but He took on him the seed of Abraham. 17 Wherefore in all things it behooved Him to be made like unto His brethren, that He might be a merciful and faithful high priest in things pertaining to God, to make reconciliation for the sins of the people.

Just as Isaiah foretold, "a virgin" conceived and brought forth that prophetic "seed" that would "bruise the head of the serpent." As both Isaiah prophesied and the angel Gabriel told Mary, this child would be called "Immanuel... which being interpreted is, God-with-us."

Isaiah 7:14 - Therefore the Lord Himself shall give you a sign; Behold, a virgin shall conceive, and bear a Son, and shall call His name Immanuel.

Matthew 1:18 - Now the birth of Jesus Christ was on this wise: When as his mother Mary was espoused to Joseph, before they came together, she was found with child of the Holy Ghost... 21 And she shall bring forth a son, and you shall call His name JESUS: for He shall save His people from their sins. 22 Now all this was done, that it might be fulfilled which was spoken of the Lord by the prophet, saying, 23 Behold, a virgin shall be with child, and shall bring forth a Son, and they shall call His name Emmanuel, which being interpreted is, God with us.

Consider a few more scriptures;

Isaiah 9:6 - For unto us a child is born, unto us a son is given: and the government shall be upon His shoulder: and His name shall be called Wonderful, Counsellor, The Mighty God, The Everlasting Father, The Prince of Peace.

Isaiah 43:10 - You are My witnesses," says the Lord, "and My servant whom I have chosen; that you may know and believe Me, and **understand that I am He** [*the child to come*]. 11 Before Me there was no God formed, neither shall there be after Me. I, even I, am the Lord; and besides Me there is no saviour... 15 I am the Lord, your Holy One, the Creator of Israel, your King.

Now compare the above verses with these.

John 8:23 - And He said unto them, You are from beneath; I am from above: you are of this world; I am not of this world. 24 I said therefore unto you, that you shall die in your sins: for **if you believe not that I am He**, you shall die in your sins. 25 Then said they unto Him, "Who are you?" And Jesus said unto them, "Even the same that I said unto you from the beginning. 26 I have many things to say and to judge of you: but He that sent Me is true; and I speak to the world those things which I have heard of Him." 27 They understood not that He spoke to them of the Father. 28 Then said Jesus unto them, "When you have lifted up the Son of man, then shall you know that **I am He**, and that I do nothing of Myself; but as My Father has taught Me, I speak these things."

John 13:19 - Now I tell you before it come, that, when it is come to pass, you may believe that **I am He**.

John 18:4 - Jesus therefore, knowing all things that should come upon Him, went forth, and said unto them, "Whom do you seek?" 5 They answered Him, "Jesus of Nazareth." Jesus says unto them, "**I am He**." And Judas also, which betrayed Him, stood with them. 6 As soon then as He had said unto them "**I am He**," they went backward, and fell to the ground. 7 Then asked He them again, "Whom do you seek?" And they said, "Jesus of Nazareth." 8 Jesus answered, "I have told you that **I am He**: if therefore you seek Me, let these go their way." 9 That the saying might be fulfilled, which He spoke, "Of them which You gave Me have I lost none."

In Jesus alone do we see the above verses fulfilled. As Paul stated, "God was manifested in the flesh." Amazingly, in His finite fleshly form as a "son of man" God's love and commitment was revealed for all heaven and earth to see. His incarnation permitted both men and angels to witness His unselfish character through the life and death of the man Jesus. Oh, what wondrous thing is this? "God in Christ" reconciling "the world unto Himself [*and*] not imputing their trespasses unto them."

II Corinthians 5:18 - And all things are of God, who has reconciled us to Himself by [*the man*] Jesus Christ, and has given to us the ministry of reconciliation; 19 To wit, that God was in Christ, reconciling the world unto Himself, not imputing their trespasses unto them; and has committed unto us the word of reconciliation.

Through the power and wisdom of His incarnation, God has revealed "unto us the mystery of His will, according to His good pleasure which He has purposed in Himself: that in the dispensation of the fullness of time He might *gather together in one* <*anakephalaiomai*> ALL things in Christ, both which are in heaven [*angels*], and which are on earth [*mankind*]; even in Him [*Jesus*]" (Ephesians 1:9, 10).

The Greek word <*anakephalaiomai*> which was translated "*gather together in one*" in Ephesians 1:10 is only used twice in scriptures. Being a compound, it proves to be a very interesting word, for the first part <*ana*> was used 16 times in scripture being variously translated as; *among* (1x), *apiece* (2x), *between* (1x), *by* (4x), *each* (1x), *every* (1x), *every man* (2x), *in the midst* (1x), *through* (2x), & *two* (1x).

The second part of the compound is the Greek word, <*kephalaioo*>, which means; *to strike on the head: -wound in the head.* In scripture this Greek word was so used but once in the following verse.

Mark 12:4 - And again he sent unto them another servant; and at him they cast stones, and **wounded him in the head** <*kephalaioo*> and sent him away shamefully handled.

That second part, <*kephalaioo*>, is of the same origin as the Greek word <*kephalaion*> which means; *a principal thing, i.e. main point; specially, an amount (of money):--the sum, summed up.*

Both words have their origin from the Greek word <*kephale*> which simply means literally or figuratively; *the head.* Thus, the original Greek compound word translated "gather together in one" conveys the sense of bringing all things and everyone together in a comprehensively correct, solidified and unshakable sense. Kind of like when a person who has been puzzled by a matter suddenly gestures by tapping themselves on the side of their head and says excitedly, "I got it! I finally understand it now!"

That is why the second place this Greek word was used in scripture it was translated with an English word to signify; know, grasp, understand & realize. Perhaps another phrase that might help convey the same concept is "Hitting the nail on the head" which is often used when something stated truly drives the point home with succinct clarity as seen below.

Romans 13:9 - For this, You shall not commit adultery, You shall not kill, You shall not steal, You shall not bear false witness, You shall not covet; and if there be any other commandment, *it-is-briefly-comprehended* <*anakephalaiomai*> in this saying, namely, You shall love your neighbor as yourself.

But not all men will embrace the Gospel of Jesus Christ or receive a love for the truth and thus not all are enabled to understand this mystery which was hidden even from the angels from the foundation of the world whereby "God was manifested in the flesh, justified in the spirit."

II Thessalonians 2:10 - ...because they received not the love of the truth, that they might be saved. 11 And for this cause God shall send them strong delusion, that they should believe a lie: 12 That they all might be damned who believed not the truth, but had pleasure in unrighteousness.

I Corinthians 1:23 - But we preach Christ crucified, unto the Jews a stumblingblock, and unto the Greeks foolishness; 24 But unto them which are called, both Jews and Greeks, Christ the power of God, and the wisdom of God.

Now we who believe do see both "the power... and the wisdom of God" in Jesus Christ. Therefore, we give "thanks unto the Father... Who has delivered us from the kingdom of darkness, and translated us unto the kingdom of His dear Son... Who is the image [*manifestation*] of the invisible God... He is before all things, and by Him all things consist. And He is the head of the body, the church: Who is The Beginning, the Firstborn from the Dead; that in all things He might have the preeminence. For it pleased the Father that in Him [*the man child*] should all fullness [*of The Mighty God*] dwell; and having made peace through the blood of His cross, by Him to reconcile all things unto Himself; by Him, I say, whether they be things in earth, or things in heaven," (Colossians 1:12-20).

In order for Jesus to qualify as the prophetic "Christ" and to fulfill all prophecy, by to necessity He had to simultaneously be both God and Man. Were Jesus not fully God and fully man He could not be what He claims to be in Revelation 22:16, both "the root and offspring of David." As the "root of David" we see Jesus Christ as "The Everlasting Father." As the "offspring of David" we see Him as the "man child" or "son" promised at the fall of Adam.

Jesus is not merely some subservient offspring of "Father God." No, in spite of how hard it is for some to believe, Jesus in His pure and ultimate essence is the Father and The Mighty God. This is not some foolish idea of my own imagination, rather what the very word of God plainly declares.

Isaiah 9:6 - For unto us a child is born, unto us a son is given: and the government shall be upon His shoulder: and His name shall be called Wonderful, Counsellor, The mighty God, The everlasting Father, The Prince of Peace.

Perhaps the most common stumbling block for people concerning Jesus' deity is an apparent inability to answer the question, "How can Jesus be the Mighty God and Everlasting Father and yet still be seen in scripture praying to the Father?"

That is both an honest and great question that has perplexed many. Nevertheless, Isaiah speaking under the unction of the Holy Spirit clearly stated that the "Prince of Peace" would be none other than "The Everlasting Father," or as some would assert "the Father of Eternity." Indeed, it is a great mystery to the finite minds of men and angels, but just because something is a mystery does not make it impossible. For a mystery is simply proof of ignorance: a lack of knowledge and understanding.

A good guideline when seeking to understand Christ, the God/man, is to remember that in His pure essence God "is a spirit," which by Jesus' own words we know that "a spirit has not flesh and bones." Therefore, God in His pure essence as a spirit is not limited to a finite visible form. Being omnipresent, He is everywhere all the time, throughout time, at the same time - past, present, future. Therefore Jesus, while locked in time and space by His human flesh, through the medium of prayer communed with His Omnipresent Spirit, "the high and lofty One that inhabits eternity."

John 4:24 - God is a Spirit: and they that worship Him must worship Him in spirit and in truth.

Luke 24:36 - And as they spoke, Jesus Himself stood in the midst of them, and said unto them, "Peace be unto you." 37 But they were terrified and affrighted, and supposed that they had seen a spirit. 38 And He said unto them, "Why are you troubled? and why do thoughts arise in your hearts? 39 Behold My hands and My feet, that it is I myself: handle me, and see; for a spirit has not flesh and bones, as you see Me have."

Isaiah 57:15 - For thus says the High and Lofty One that inhabits eternity, whose name is Holy; I dwell in the high and holy place, with him also that is of a contrite and humble spirit, to revive the spirit of the humble, and to revive the heart of the contrite ones.

Now consider this, if it were possible for you to go back in time, even just one minute, you could both see and be with yourself. You could even sit across from yourself and carry on a conversation. But would that make you two people? Certainly, at that very moment, it would seem as if there were in fact two of you. Nevertheless, in reality you are still only one person; one in heart, one in mind. But yet having escaped the parameters of time you now appear as two, both being in one place at the same time.

It would be the unique ability to escape time that gave you the ability to be in two places simultaneously. You, from a distant place or future time could literally go and counsel yourself as to what is occurring elsewhere, or even that which is yet to come to pass. Interesting concept, right?

Yet this is literally what Jesus expressed to Nicodemus, "No man has ascended up to heaven, but He that came down from heaven, even the Son of Man which is in heaven," (John 3:13). Jesus was standing right there with Nicodemus affirming to him that even at that very moment He "is in heaven."

It is because of this unique aspect of God's omnipresence that He foreknew those who "should be saved" even from the very foundations of the world.

Isaiah 41:4 - Who has wrought and done it, calling the generations from the beginning? I the LORD, the first, and with the last; **I am He**.

Acts 2:47 - ...And the Lord added to the church daily such as should be saved.

Isaiah 46:9 – "Remember the former things of old: for I am God, and there is none else; I am God, and there is none like Me, 10 Declaring the end from the beginning, and from ancient times the things that are not yet done," saying, "My counsel shall stand, and I will do all My pleasure."

Isaiah 48:3 - I have declared the former things from the beginning; and they went forth out of my mouth, and I showed them; I did them suddenly, and they came to pass... 5 I have even from the beginning declared it to you; before it came to pass I showed it to you: lest you should say, "Mine idol has done them, and my graven image, and my molten image, has commanded them."

At Athens, the Apostle Paul encouraged the men there to "seek the Lord [*Jesus*], if haply they might feel after Him, and find Him, though He be not far from every one of us. **For in Him we live and move** and have our very being," (Acts 17:27, 28).

Likewise, in Psalm 139, David reasons with God saying, "Where shall I go from Your Spirit? Or where shall I flee from Your presence? If I ascend up into heaven, You are there. If I make my bed in hell, behold, You are there. If I take the wings of morning and dwell in the uttermost parts of the sea, even there shall Your hand lead me and Your right hand hold me," (Verses 7-10).

Consider once again God's greatness in His words to Jeremiah.

Jeremiah 23:24 – "Am I a God at hand, says the LORD, and not a God afar off? Can any hide himself in secret places that I shall not see him?" says the LORD. "Do not I fill heaven and earth?" says the LORD.

Thus, we can see the omnipresence of the "eternal, immortal, invisible, the only wise God." Now consider the Apostle John's words as he explains the great relationship we can have with the Father and Christ if "we walk in the light."

I John 1:3 - That which we have seen and heard declare we unto you, that you also may have fellowship with us: and truly our fellowship is with the Father, and with His Son Jesus Christ. 4 And these things write we unto you, that your joy may be full. 5 This then is the message which we have heard of Him, and declare unto you, that God is light, and in Him is no darkness at all. 6 If we say that we have fellowship with Him, and walk in darkness, we lie, and do not the truth: 7 But if we walk in the light, as He is in the light, we have fellowship one with another, and the blood of Jesus Christ His Son cleanses us from all sin.

This walking "in the light" is more intimate than the "in Him we live and move and have our very being" which Paul spoke of to the men at Athens. This "IN" the Apostle John speaks of is even much more than some hyper-spiritual concept concerning the "Christian position." This "IN" is the intimate communion all believers are supposed to be living in with God through Christ Jesus. I stress this not to shame anyone who may realize they are lacking this personal familiarity with God, but rather to motivate and to stir up both your faith and faithfulness; for this intimacy is only possible for those who have made a conscious resolve to no longer "walk not after the flesh, but after the Spirit."

Romans 8:1 - There is therefore now no condemnation to them which are in Christ Jesus, who walk not after the flesh, but after the Spirit. 2 For the law of the Spirit of life in Christ Jesus has made me free from the law of sin and death. 3 For what the law could not do, in that it was weak through the flesh, God sending His own Son in the likeness of sinful flesh, and for sin, condemned sin in the flesh: 4 That the righteousness of the law might be fulfilled in us, who walk not after the flesh, but after the Spirit. 5 For they that are after the flesh do mind the things of the flesh; but they that are after the Spirit the things of the Spirit. 6 For to be carnally minded is death; but to be spiritually minded is life and peace.

Surely, we all want "the law of the Spirit of life which is in Christ Jesus" to make us "free from the law of sin and death." But do we really understand who this "Spirit" is? It is the "Spirit of Christ" of course; and isn't it "IN" Him whom we want to be intimately familiar with? And do we recognize Paul is cautioning us that we must "mind" Him and "walk after" Him if "the righteousness of the law might be fulfilled in us?" Nevertheless, many Christians go about their lives as if they don't believe Paul when he warns us that "to be carnally minded is death; but to be SPIRITually minded is life and peace."

Romans 8:9 - But you are not in the flesh, but in the **SPIRIT**, if so be that the **SPIRIT OF GOD** dwell in you. Now if any man has not the **SPIRIT OF CHRIST**, he is none of His.

Furthermore this "Spirit of Christ" is none other than the Holy Spirit. Due to "the MYSTERY of Christ" a common mistake many believers make is they perceive the phrase "Holy Spirit" to be a proper name, when in actually it is a precise description of God. He's holy and in all purity of essence He is a spirit. Therefore, God alone can properly be called a "Holy Spirit."

Before we continue let's look at some more scriptures referencing this "mystery."

Romans 16:25 - Now to Him that is of power to establish you according to my gospel, and the preaching of Jesus Christ, according to the revelation of the mystery, which was kept secret since the world began.

I Corinthians 2:7 - But we speak the wisdom of God in a mystery, even the hidden wisdom, which God ordained before the world unto our glory.

Ephesians 3:3 - How that by revelation He made known unto me the mystery; (as I wrote afore in few words, 4 Whereby, when you read, you may understand my knowledge in the mystery of Christ).

Colossians 2:2 - That their hearts might be comforted, being knit together in love, and unto all riches of the full assurance of understanding, to the acknowledgement of the mystery of God, and [*even*] of the Father and of Christ.

Colossians 4:3 - Withal praying also for us, that God would open unto us a door of utterance, to speak the mystery of Christ, for which I am also in bonds.

I Timothy 3:16 - And without controversy great is the mystery of godliness: God was manifest in the flesh, justified in the Spirit, seen of angels, preached unto the Gentiles, believed on in the world, received up into glory.

God Spoke

Now let's look at a few scriptures that help to open up this mystery further and will give us all a greater appreciation for the wisdom, power and love of God has given us in and through Christ Jesus the Lord.

Hebrew 1:1 - **God**, who at sundry times and in diverse manners **spoke** in time past unto the fathers **by the prophets**, 2 Has in these last days spoken unto us **by His Son**, whom He has appointed heir of all things, by whom also He made the worlds; 3 Who being the brightness of His glory, and the express image of His person, and upholding all things by the word of His power, when He had by Himself purged our sins, sat down on the right hand of the Majesty on high.

Note the words in bold type, "God, spoke, by the prophets, by His Son." Let's continue.

II Peter 1:21 - For the prophecy came not in old time by the will of man: but **holy men of God spoke as they were moved by the Holy Ghost**.

Here we see "God" who "spoke, by the prophets" in Hebrews 1:1-2 speaking by "holy men of God as they were moved by the Holy Ghost."

Same God, same prophets, same Spirit, all recorded in God's Holy Scripture.

Again, let's continue;

I Peter 1:10 - Of which salvation **the prophets** have enquired and searched diligently, who **prophesied of the grace that should come** unto you: 11 Searching what, or what manner of time **the Spirit of Christ which was in them did signify**, when it testified beforehand the sufferings of Christ, and the glory that should follow.

These verses all say the same thing, God has spoken through men: for the "**prophets**" through which "**God... spoke**" as they "**were moved by the Holy Ghost,**" spoke that which "**the Spirit of Christ which was in them did signify**." Just as surely the Holy Spirit of Christ was in the prophets, it was God Himself, even Emmanuel, who was in this man-child called Jesus Christ.

Matthew 1:23 - Behold, a virgin shall be with child, and shall bring forth a son, and they shall call His name Emmanuel, which being interpreted is, God with us.

II Corinthians 5:18 - And all things are of God, who has reconciled us to Himself by [*the man*] Jesus Christ and has given to us the ministry of reconciliation; 19 To wit, that God was in Christ, reconciling the world unto Himself, not imputing their trespasses unto them; and has committed unto us the word of reconciliation.

II Corinthians 3:17 - Now the Lord [*Jesus*] is that Spirit: and where the Spirit of the Lord is there is liberty.

In light of all these scriptures I would hope all could agree that when the Bible speaks of the Holy Spirit, the Spirit of God, and the Spirit of Christ, that it is speaking of the same Spirit. For scripture tells us there is only "one Spirit."

Ephesians 4:3 - Endeavoring to keep the unity of the Spirit in the bond of peace. 4 There is one body, and **one Spirit**, even as you are called in one hope of your calling; 5 **One Lord**, one faith, one baptism, 6 **One God and Father of all**, Who is above all, and through all, and in you all.

I Corinthians 12:11 - But all these works that **one and the selfsame Spirit**, dividing to every man severally as He will. 12 For as the body is one, and has many members, and all the members of that one body, being many, are one body: **so also is Christ**. 13 For by **one**

Spirit are we all baptized into one body, whether we be Jews or Gentiles, whether we be bond or free; and have been all made to drink into **one Spirit**.

Since by the word of God we know there is only "one Spirit," when Paul states that God was "justified in the Spirit," it should be understood that it was the Holy Spirit of the "eternal, immortal, invisible, the **ONLY** wise God" Almighty that was "manifested in the flesh" of the man Jesus.

I Timothy 1:17 - Now unto the King eternal, immortal, invisible, the only wise God, be honor and glory for ever and ever. Amen.

I Timothy 3:16 - ...God was manifest in the flesh, justified in the Spirit, seen of angels, preached unto the Gentiles, believed on in the world, received up into glory.

I Timothy 2:5 For there is one God, and one mediator between God and men, the man Christ Jesus;

Galatians 3:20 - Now a mediator is not a mediator of one, but God is one.

Though this mystery was hidden from the foundation of the world, God still put forth a riddle to us in the Book of Proverbs which He will sooner or later require everyone to answer.

Proverbs 30:4 - Who has ascended up into heaven, or descended? Who has gathered the wind in His fist? Who has bound the waters in a garment? Who has established all the ends of the earth? What is His name? And what is His Son's name, if you can tell?

This riddle is one that men all over the world have long sought to answer. And in their search for an answer, neither their own imagination, nor the adversary has failed to provide a wide array of doctrines to select from. Such is why Jesus asked a similar question of His disciples, so don't think that He will not ask the same of you...

Luke 9:18 - And it came to pass, as He was alone praying, His disciples were with Him: and He asked them, saying, "Who do the people say that I am?" 19 They answering said, "John the Baptist; but some say, Elias; and others say, that one of the old prophets is risen again." 20 He said unto them, "But whom say you that I am?"

We cannot afford to be wrong in our response, we must "know in whom" we believe. Fortunately,

He who has asked the question is also willing to provide the answer to it.

Isaiah 43:10 - You are my witnesses, says the LORD, and My servant whom I have chosen: **that you may know and believe Me, and understand that I am He**: before Me there was no God formed, neither shall there be after Me. 11 I, even I, am the LORD; and beside Me there is no savior.

I Timothy 4:10 - For therefore we both labor and suffer reproach, because we trust in the living **God, who is the Savior of all men**, specially of those that believe.

II Timothy 1:8 - Be you not therefore ashamed of the testimony of our Lord, nor of me His prisoner: but be you partaker of the afflictions of the gospel according to the power of God; 9 Who has saved us and called us with an holy calling. Not according to our works, but according to His own purpose and grace which was given us in Christ Jesus before the world began. 10 But, **now is made manifest by the appearing of our Savior Jesus Christ**, Who has abolished death and has brought life and immortality to light through the gospel. 11 Whereunto I am appointed a preacher, and an apostle, and a teacher of the Gentiles. 12 For the which cause I also suffer these things: nevertheless, I am not ashamed: for I know whom I have believed and am persuaded that He is able to keep that which I have committed unto Him against that day.

Titus 1:1 - Paul, a servant of God, and an apostle of Jesus Christ, according to the faith of God's elect, and the acknowledging of the truth which is after godliness; 2 In hope of eternal life, which God, that cannot lie, promised before the world began; 3 But has in due times manifested His word through preaching, which is committed unto me according to the commandment of **God our Savior**; 4 To Titus, mine own son after the common faith: Grace, mercy, and peace, from **God the Father and the Lord Jesus Christ our Savior**.

Titus 2:10 - Not purloining, but shewing all good fidelity; that they may adorn **the doctrine of God our Savior** in all things. 11 **For the grace of God that brings salvation has appeared to all men**, 12 Teaching us that, denying ungodliness and worldly lusts, we should live soberly, righteously, and godly, in this present world; 13 **Looking for that blessed hope, and the glorious appearing of the great God and our Savior Jesus Christ**; 14 Who gave Himself for us, that He might redeem us from all iniquity, and purify unto Himself a peculiar people, zealous of good works.

Titus 3:4 - But after that the kindness and love of **God our Savior** toward man appeared, 5 Not by works of righteousness which we have done, but according to His mercy He saved us, by the washing of regeneration, and renewing of the Holy Ghost; 6 Which He shed on us abundantly through **Jesus Christ our Savior**; 7 That being justified by His grace, we should be made heirs according to the hope of eternal life. 8 This is a faithful saying, and these things I will that you affirm constantly, that **they which have believed in God** might be careful to maintain good works. These things are good and profitable unto men.

Isaiah 43:12 – "I have declared, and have saved, and I have showed, when there was no strange god among you: therefore, you are My witnesses," says the LORD, "That I am God. 13 Yea, before the day was I am He; and there is none that can deliver out of My hand: I will work, and who shall let it? 14 Thus says the LORD, your redeemer, the Holy One of Israel… 15 I am the LORD, your Holy One, the Creator of Israel, your King."

John 10:27 – "My sheep hear My voice, and I know them, and they follow Me: 28 And I give unto them eternal life; and they shall never perish, neither shall any man pluck them out of My hand. 29 My Father, which gave them Me, is greater than all; and no man is able to pluck them out of my Father's hand. 30 I and my Father are one." 31 Then the Jews took up stones again to stone Him. 32 Jesus answered them, "Many good works have I showed you from My Father; for which of those works do you stone Me?" 33 The Jews answered Him, saying, "For a good work we stone You not; but for blasphemy; and because that You, being a man, make Yourself God."

We have been warned to "believe not every spirit [*be it of man or angel*]," and are instructed to "try the spirits whether they are of God; because many false prophets are gone out into the world." Here's how the scriptures say we should try the spirits that we might know those that are of God.

I John 4:1 - Beloved, believe not every spirit, but try the spirits whether they are of God: because many false prophets are gone out into the world. 2 Hereby know you the Spirit of God: Every spirit that confesses that Jesus Christ is come in the flesh is of God: 3

And every spirit that confesses not that Jesus Christ is come in the flesh is not of God: and this is that spirit of antichrist, whereof you have heard that it should come; and even now already is it in the world.

Now take a moment and consider the lasting effect of Jesus Christ upon humanity. Now really, who but an ignorant person or a lying fool would deny that a man named "Jesus" ever existed? Even historians who do not subscribe to the beliefs of Christianity readily acknowledge Jesus' existence. Likewise, religions which are diabolically opposed to the Christian faith acknowledge that historically there was a man named Jesus who claimed to be the Christ; some even recognizing Him as a prophet. Due to the overwhelming evidence, any person with a measurable and honest intellect must acknowledge that not only did such a man "come in the flesh," but that He was crucified in the flesh as well. Nevertheless, these two facts are not what the Apostle John was talking about.

The spirit of antichrist is not "anti-Jesus came in the flesh," nor is it "anti-Jesus the subservient offspring of God come in the flesh." Amazingly, neither is the spirit of antichrist "anti-god." Quite to the contrary, to many people's surprise the Bible tells us this spirit of antichrist is really "pro-god." It just is not "pro the true and living God."

See the Bible says "that man of sin" will exalt himself "so that he AS GOD sits in the temple of God, showing himself that he is God," (II Thessalonians 2:2, 4). Yet this "he" could not do if people truly knew, understood, and comprehended that Jesus Christ was God. Therefore, the nature of the spirit of antichrist is to be anti-truth, meaning "Anti-Jesus Christ, the Almighty God our Savior come in the flesh."

Jesus said, "Take heed that no man deceives you. For many will come in My name, saying I am the Christ; and shall deceive many" (Matthew 24:4, 5). These are men who will acknowledge both the life and death of Jesus, and openly admit that He was the foretold and promised deliverer that would come, a great prophet, and even the Christ. Yet their definition of "the Christ" is contrary to that of God's.

Countless so-called Christian leaders in Christendom nowadays reject the scriptural evidence that Jesus Christ was "The Mighty God, The Everlasting Father" come in the flesh, (Isaiah 9:6). In one breath they acknowledge that Jesus is the "Prince of Peace," but with the next breath boldly declare that He cannot be the Everlasting Father.

51

II John 7 - This is a deceiver and an antichrist. Whosoever transgresses and abides not in the doctrine of Christ has not God... 9 He that abides in the doctrine of Christ, he has both the [*Everlasting*] Father and the Son.

Notice the singularity of the word "doctrine" in II John 9. It is singular because John was not referring to the many doctrines, or teachings, which were given to us through Jesus's earthly ministry. No, John was referring to that one singular doctrine which is the foundation of true Christianity. It is the teaching concerning "Who is Jesus Christ." The Bible calls this teaching the "Doctrine of Christ" and God will not permit this doctrine to be changed; those who do so will certainly suffer severe and eternal consequences. Thus, the Apostle John warned us that "if any come unto you and bring not THIS doctrine [*but a different teaching of whom Christ is*], receive him not into your house, neither bid him God speed: for he that bids him God speed is a partaker of his evil deeds," (II John 10, 11).

I John 2:22 - Who is a liar but he that denies Jesus is the Christ? He is antichrist that denies the Father and the Son [*are one God*]. 22 Whosoever denies the [*Isaiah 9:6*] Son, the same has not the [*Everlasting*] Father: but he that acknowledges the Son has the [*Everlasting*] Father also.

Why is it that he who acknowledges the Son has the Father also? Because in spirit "They" are the same; and scriptures say that if this truth be hid, it is hidden to them that are lost.

II Corinthians 4:3 - But if our gospel be hid, it is hid to them that are lost: 4 In whom the god of this world has blinded the minds of them which believe not, lest the light of the glorious gospel of Christ, who is the image of God, should shine unto them. 5 For we preach not ourselves, but Christ Jesus the Lord; and ourselves your servants for Jesus' sake. 6 For God, who commanded the light to shine out of darkness, has shined in our hearts, to give the light of the knowledge of the glory of God in the face of Jesus Christ.

The truths presented thus far are the foundation of the "Doctrine of Christ" and the very heart of the Gospel. It is upon this "rock" that the true church of Jesus Christ was founded.

Therefore, if a person is ignorant, or disbelieving of this truth, it is because they are blind to the true light of the glory of God in the face of Jesus Christ and have likely embraced "another

Jesus" and are believing in "another gospel" and following "another spirit."

II Corinthians 11:4 - If indeed someone is coming to preach another Jesus, whom I did not preach, or you are receiving a Spirit other than you once received, or another gospel which you did not accept before, you would do well to bear with me. (*Montgomery's New Testament*)

Matthew 7:21 - "Not everyone who says to Me, 'Lord, Lord,' shall enter the kingdom of heaven, but he who does the will of My Father in heaven. 22 "Many will say to Me in that day, 'Lord, Lord, have we not prophesied in Your name, cast out demons in Your name, and done many wonders in Your name?' 23 "And then I will declare to them, 'I never knew you; depart from Me you who practice lawlessness!'

Matthew 24:5 For many will come in My name [*the name of Jesus*], saying, [*or acknowledging that*] "I am Christ," and [*yet they*] will deceive many.

Many preachers preach that these are people coming and professing themselves to be the christ; but the word "christ" is not a name. "Christ" is a prophesied and anointed position that only Jesus can fill.

WHAT WAS GOD JUSTIFIED OF?

Now is a good time to explore what the word "justified" means. The Greek word in 1 Timothy 3:16 translated "Justified" is "dikaioo" which comes from the root word "dikaios." Let's look at their definitions.

Dikaios - equitable (in character or act); by implication, innocent, holy (absolutely or relatively): just, meet, right (eous).

Dikaioo - to render (i.e. show or regard as) just or innocent.

Merriam Webster defined *justified* as "to be shown just, right, and to have functioned in accord with good reason. To be freed from blame; declared guiltless; acquitted; absolved." By these definitions we could easily say, "To be justified is to be vindicated of false accusation by the revealed, proven, and witnessed (seen and heard) facts." If this is true, then what were the accusations of which God was vindicated of through His incarnation and who made them?

The first recorded accusation in the Bible was against God. When and how did it happen? Well, Eve was in the garden one day when a serpent asked her, "Has God said you should not eat of every tree in the garden?" Eve's reply was, "We may eat the fruit of every tree in the garden; except the tree in the middle of the garden, God said, you shall not eat of it, neither shall you touch it, lest you die." And the serpent said unto Eve, "You shall not surely die: for God knows that in the day you eat it your eyes shall be open and you shall be as gods, knowing good and evil," (Genesis 3:1-24).

Here we see the devil, via the serpent, asserting that God was a liar by his saying, "You shall not surely die." Satan further implied that the reason God did not want Adam and Eve to eat of the tree was because God was selfish and did not want any other gods around, for "God knows... you shall be as gods," (Genesis 3:5).

For all intents and purposes, Satan accused God of being both a deceiver and lover of self; and if God was selfish, then He must be a sinner as well. It was this arrogant manner of defiance, deceitfulness of sin, and blasphemy against God and His character that provoked Him to not spare those "angels that sinned, but cast them down to hell, and delivered them into chains of darkness, to be reserved unto judgment," (II Peter 2:4).

For Satan and the other angels who were eyewitnesses to His majesty to commit these manners of sin, there could be no forgiveness. For "Whosoever speaks against the Holy Ghost, it shall not be forgiven him, neither in this world, neither in the world to come," (Matthew 10:25).

As Christians, we know Satan's accusations are false, yet in them we can see both the jealousy and extreme hatred he holds towards God. Interestingly, there are scriptures that may very well reveal to us that the incident in the garden may not be the first time Satan accused God of these things and greedily hoarding the throne. This we'll discover as we look into the devil's beginning.

THE DEVIL'S BEGINNING

I John 3:8 - He that commits sin is of the devil; for the devil sinned from the beginning. For this purpose, the Son of God was manifested, that He might destroy the works of the devil.

When the Apostle John said, "The devil sinned from the beginning," have you ever thought just what "beginning" was he referring to? Since the devil was perfect in all his ways from the day that he was created, it would have to be from the beginning of his negative conversion. What does that mean? Well, let's look at those texts of scripture in the Bible that offer us insight into his former state.

Ezekiel 28:13 - You had been in Eden the garden of God; every precious stone was your covering, the sardius, topaz, and the diamond, the beryl, the onyx, and the jasper, the sapphire, the emerald, and the carbuncle, and gold: the workmanship of your tabrets and of thy pipes was prepared in you in the day that you were created. 14 You are the anointed cherub that covers; and I have set you so: you were upon the holy mountain of God; you have walked up and down in the midst of the stones of fire. 15 You were perfect in your ways from the day that you were created, till iniquity was found in you. 16 By the multitude of your merchandise they have filled the midst of you with violence, and you have sinned: therefore, I will cast you as profane out of the mountain of God: and I will destroy you, O covering cherub, from the midst of the stones of fire. 17 Your heart was lifted up because of your beauty, you have corrupted your wisdom by reason of your brightness: I will cast you to the ground, I will lay you before kings, that they may behold you.

Isaiah 14:12 - How you have fallen from heaven, O Lucifer, son of the morning! are you cut down to the ground, which did weaken the nations! 13 For you have said in your heart, "I will ascend into heaven, I will exalt my throne above the stars of God: I will sit also upon the mount of the congregation, in the sides of the north: 14 I will ascend above the heights of the clouds; I will be like the Most High." 15 Yet you shall be brought down to hell, to the sides of the pit.

To be forthright, there are some commentators who have rejected the notion that either of these two passages have anything to do with the fall of Lucifer. They assert Ezekiel's prophecy was specifically speaking of the king of Tyrus, and only of the king of Tyrus. However, that perspective offers no clarity to certain points in the prophecy, as the king of Tyrus was never "in Eden the garden of God," nor was he ever an "anointed cherub." Certainly, it must be openly acknowledged as well that the king of Tyrus was born and not "created" as referenced in the prophecy.

Likewise, some regard Isaiah's prophecy as solely an addressment of the sins of the king of Babylon. Yet Isaiah, as did Ezekiel, prophesied by the same Holy Spirit "unto men to edification, and exhortation, and comfort," (I Corinthians 14:3-5). These two prophecies do indeed focus pointedly upon these two kings; because like Satan they too exalted themselves beyond their appointed realm of power and influence.

Thus, while those prophecies may indeed historically shed some light on these two kings' personal sins, it is Satan's sin and fall that becomes their eventual focal point; as if a spot light has been placed on Satan himself. For all pride and rebellion stems from that point in pre-Adamic history when sin in the heavens was first committed as the anointed cherub's own heart turned away from God and he became a lover of self.

Deuteronomy 30:17 - But if your heart turn away, so that you will not hear, but shall be drawn away, and worship other gods, and serve them.

James 1:14 - But every man is tempted, when he is drawn away of his own lust, and enticed.

Self Esteem

Thus, in light of those specific references within these prophecies that address Lucifer and his fall, it is difficult to reject the notion that both Ezekiel and Isaiah's prophecies were given through the Holy Spirit for a historical record of the fall of the anointed cherub. For through them we have been given insight into the origin of all sin, i.e. SELF-esteem. For unless one knows where they came from and who they truly are and in whom they believe, pride will be stirred up in their hearts. Then it is only a matter of time before they will begin to esteem themselves as deserving of the respect, praise, and admiration of others. For this very reason Paul told Timothy not to place a novice into a position of leadership before he has been proven to be mature and well established in the Lord's service and firmly rooted and grounded in love.

I Timothy 3:2 - A bishop then must be blameless, the husband of one wife, vigilant, sober, of good behavior, given to hospitality, apt to teach; 3 Not given to wine, no striker, not greedy of filthy lucre; but patient, not a brawler, not covetous; 4 One that rules well his own house, having his children in subjection with all gravity; 5 (For if a man know not how to rule his own house, how shall he take care of the church of God?) 6 Not a novice, lest being lifted up with pride he fall into the condemnation of the devil.

That phrase, "fall into the condemnation of the devil," does not imply what many people perceive. Many think Paul is saying that the devil will only end up condemning the novice if he indeed becomes prideful.

While it is obvious that the devil will indeed try to tempt and thus bring condemnation upon the novice, we must remember that God alone is the one who will ultimately condemn all unrepentant sinners. Rather, the Apostle Paul was warning Timothy that just as Satan was condemned for his pride, so too would the novice be if he were hastily placed in a position where he could be enticed and "lifted up with pride." For from the beginning of all sin, "pride goes before destruction and a haughty spirit before a fall."

In this light we can see how both the king of Tyrus and the king of Babylon displayed those attributes which originated in Satan, the ultimate chief of all sinners. As it had transpired with Satan, they too had allowed their positions and wealth to seduce them into believing a lie.

For although God had given those positions of honor to them, these two kings had allowed their hearts to get puffed up and they began to think it was of their own power and wisdom that they had become mighty. They began to think that of their own selves they were great and special; when in reality they were nothing. The deceitfulness of their sins had ensnared them. Their positions and power came not by their wisdom or doing, for God had given it to them. Therefore, their postures should have been that which was full of humility and thankfulness, not pride.

Let's look at Ezekiel's and Isaiah's account of the devil's narcissistic heart.

Ezekiel 28:17 – Your heart was lifted up because of your beauty, you have corrupted your wisdom by reason of your brightness.

Isaiah 14:13 - For you have said in thine heart, I will ascend unto heaven, I will exalt my throne above the stars of God: I will also sit upon the congregation, in the sides of the north: 14 I will ascend above the clouds: I will be like the Most High.

Here we see the deceitful progression of SELF-esteem. For it caused Satan to view himself as superior to the rest of God's angelic beings, stirring up in his heart a lust and ambition to place himself above them as he proclaimed his ultimate ambition, "I will exalt my throne above the stars of God:" the stars being symbolic of God's angels as in the verse below.

Revelation 12:4 - And his tail drew the third part of the stars of heaven and did cast them to the earth: and the dragon stood before the woman which was ready to be delivered, for to devour her child as soon as it was born.

However, his self-absorbed egotistical heart could never be content with just rising above his peers, for he says, "I will be like the Most High." Mesmerized by his own beauty, Satan had become a lover of self and believed he was entitled to the same admiration, praise, and worship as God, the very Creator of his beauty. But God is worthy of all the glory "inasmuch as he who has built the house has more honor than the house."

Romans 1:24 - Wherefore God also gave them up to uncleanness through the lusts of their own hearts... 25 Who changed the truth of God into a lie and worshipped and served the creature more than the Creator, Who is blessed forever. Amen.

Self-esteem will always lead to the same end, humiliation and destruction. Sure, like many sins in their early stages, it can make one feel good, but only temporarily. Therefore, because of his SELF-esteem Satan had corrupted his wisdom and forfeited both his position with God and soiled his God-given beauty. Any beauty he now has is only a projected illusion, a covering for his nakedness as it were with mere fig leaves. Thus, because Satan had sought to honor himself instead of God his Creator, he was therefore condemned. This is what Paul was referring to when he warned the novice might "fall into the condemnation of the devil."

Ezekiel 28:17 - Your heart was lifted up because of your beauty, you corrupted your wisdom by reason of your brightness: I will cast you to the ground, I will lay you before kings, that they may behold you. 18 You have defiled your sanctuaries by the multitude of your iniquities, and by the iniquity of your merchandise. Therefore, will I bring forth a fire from the midst of you, it shall devour you, and I will bring you to ashes upon the earth in the sight of all them that behold you. 19 All they that know you among the people shall be astonished at you: you shall be a terror, and never shall you be any more.

Isaiah 14:15 - Yet you shall be brought down to hell, to the sides of the pit. 16 They that see you shall narrowly look upon you, and consider you, saying, "Is this the man that made the earth to tremble, that did shake kingdoms; 17 That made the world as a wilderness, and destroyed the cities thereof; that opened not the house of his prisoners?"

THE DEVIL IN HEAVEN

In those verses we can see God not only made an accurate assessment of Satan's heart, but He had condemned and sentenced him as well. Therefore, the following two questions arise.

> 1. Why then, if Satan was already condemned, was he there loose in the garden seducing Adam and Eve?

> 2. Why, after being sentenced to hell, was he still permitted back into the heavenly throne room?

Perhaps you've never considered these questions before, but certainly they are valid questions in light of the verses we have just looked at. To strengthen the validity of those questions let's look at scriptures in Job that seem to present Satan, who obviously refused to be subject to God's will, as being able to come and go wherever he wished. However, his liberty was really a witness to his lawlessness; and his "free spirit" nothing more than an arrogant and rebellious spirit that dared even to approach the very throne of God!

> Job 1:6 - Now there was a day when the sons of God came to present themselves before the LORD, and Satan came also among them. 7 And the LORD said unto Satan, "From where

are you coming?" Then Satan answered the LORD, and said, "From going to and fro in the earth, and from walking up and down in it".

The passage of scripture above continues with Satan accusing Job of only serving God for His protection and blessings. (Of how many Christians today could this accusation actually be proven true?) Nevertheless, God's response was not to react to Satan's accusation with His own finger pointing and calling Satan a liar. Rather, He allowed Satan to try Job, knowing that through his coming afflictions righteous Job would prove Satan to be a liar. For this reason, God allowed Satan to literally take everything Job had, except his wife. Yet get this, Job continued to worship God and to bless His name!

Next, Satan accused Job of only serving God for his good health. Again, to disprove his lies, God permitted Satan to afflict Job near unto death.

Job 2:3 - And the LORD said unto Satan, "Have you considered My servant Job, that there is none like him in the earth, a perfect and an upright man, one that fears God, and hates evil? He still holds fast his integrity, even though you move Me against him, to destroy him without cause." 4 And Satan answered the LORD, and said, "Skin for skin, yea, all that a man has will he give for his life. 5 But put forth

Your hand now, and touch his bone and his flesh, and he will curse You to Your face." 6 And the LORD said unto Satan, "Behold, he is in your hand; but save his life."

7 So went Satan forth from the presence of the LORD, and smote Job with sore boils from the sole of his foot unto his crown. 8 And he took him a potsherd to scrape himself therewith; and he sat down among the ashes. 9 Then said his wife unto him, "Do you still retain your integrity? Curse God and die." 10 But he said unto her, "You speak as one of the foolish women speaks. What? Shall we only receive good at the hand of God, and shall we not receive evil?" In all this did not Job sin with his lips.

What can be seen in all this are two things; first, the devil falsely accusing the righteous, and secondly, the righteous abstaining from reactionary and verbal sins. Much to the contrary, we see righteous Job even in the midst of his adversity remaining committed to trusting and serving God.

Job 13:15 - Though He slay me, yet will I trust in Him: but I will maintain mine own ways before Him.

Still, all this takes us back to the question, "Why did Satan have liberty to come before God in light of the judgment levied against him?"

To make this mystery even more intriguing, let's add a third question, "Why, in light of God's judgment, would part of the angelic host choose to side with the devil?"

Answer, (at least the only one which seems to make any sense and fits the devil's obvious disputatious pattern as we witnessed in scripture), the devil probably cunningly argued his defense before God and the heavenly host; and sadly "the jury" as it were was left divided.

Perhaps, Satan argumentatively began his defense calling for a comparison of his own beauty and brightness to that of God's-

"What profound visible difference is there between God and me; that He alone should be worshipped? Furthermore, if God says it is iniquity for me to sit upon a throne, why then is it not sin for Him? Is there a double standard here in heaven?

"If God does whatever He wants, then why is it that we cannot as well? Does God ask or seek our approval, why then do we need to have His?

How then, if simply because I too wish to sit on a throne, can He declare me to be a sinner worthy of hell's torment? By what standard, His own?

"If this all is true, then by His own judgment, would not God deserve the same? For is not God doing that which He Himself has now condemned me for by simply wanting to be like Him? How can this be justice, that for such I am now declared to be wrong and condemned to have fire devour me? How in all this can God be right?"

What blasphemy! Nevertheless, this harmonizes with those accusations Satan made earlier to Eve. "FOR GOD KNOWS... YOU SHALL BE GODS." Satan brazenly insinuated that it was due to God being egotistical and self-centered that He refused to let Adam and Eve eat of the tree; yet Satan knew if he could get them to eat of the fruit in an attempt to become "gods" then God would condemn them as well. Therefore, it is not hard to envision this arrogant creature consumed with envy arguing this same slander before the heavenly host.

"God's not willing to share the mount. Who's He kidding? All He wants is to sit up there, high and lofty, and demanding we all worship Him. A little too much self-esteem I'd say. Can it really be fair for God to send me to hell simply because I wanted to be like Him? It's not like I wanted His throne, just my own. I simply wanted to be LIKE the Most High, NOT THE MOST HIGH."

Whatever his argument was, Satan's reasoning had to be at the least powerfully enticing, if not convincing; for a considerable part of the heavenly host embraced his lies as plausible and elected to side with him. Regardless his argument, his desire to become a god to the other angels became a reality as a third of the angels were swept away in his revolt against the Lord God Almighty.

As the heavenly vision in Revelation 12 illustrates, the dragon "drew a third part of the stars of heaven" down to earth in attempt to kill Jesus at the time of His birth. Verse seven serves as a witness that Satan had indeed won a measurable allegiance from the fallen angels; as scripture states they became "his angels" and were now willfully partaking in his sin!

Revelation 12:4 - And his tail drew the third part of the stars of heaven and did cast them to the earth: and the dragon stood before the woman which was ready to be delivered, for to devour her child as soon as it was born. 5 And she brought forth a man child, who was to rule all nations with a rod of iron: and her child was caught up unto God, and to His throne. 6 And the woman fled into the wilderness, where she has a place prepared of God, that they should feed her there a thousand two hundred and sixty days. 7 And there was war in heaven: Michael and his angels fought against the dragon; and **the dragon fought and his angels**, 8 And prevailed not; neither was their place found any more in heaven. 9 And the great dragon was cast out, that old serpent, called the Devil, and Satan, which deceives the whole world: he was cast out into the earth, and his angels were cast out with him.

The angels who sided with Satan did so because they loved his wicked ideology more than God's holiness. As he did with Eve, can we not see how Satan might have as well proposed to the angels a life equal to God's in which they should be answerable to no one. Did he in his craftiness manage to arouse a "pride of [one's own] life" and stir up a lust for SELF-esteem? For it seems at some point the fallen angels had become slaves to their sinful envy; having hearts that both despised and coveted the very majesty of God!

These angels embraced Satan's idiot-ology. By allowing themselves to be seduced by his "deceivableness of unrighteousness" they too fell into "the condemnation of the devil." Having rejected the "love of the truth" God gave them over to Satan's "strong delusion that they should believe a lie. That they all might be damned who believed not the truth but had pleasure in unrighteousness."

Satan's accusations had shaken the whole of God's creation. No angel could escape the effect of Satan's lies, that God does whatever He wants irrespective of others and unilaterally condemns those who would seek to exercise the same "freedom" or "right." Nevertheless, most of the angels were steadfast and kept their trust in God and remained loyal; emotionally unsettled maybe, but loyal to their Creator nonetheless.

But this all brings us to another question; why didn't the Almighty God simply wink His eye or close His hand and simply do away with Satan and all those rebellious angels? Certainly, just as easily as they were spoken into creation they could have been erased or destroyed. But even though God had declared His judgment against the fallen angels, He nevertheless delayed the execution of His judgment against them.

The answer abides within the nature of God, for He is a God of love who champions indisputable truth. Thus, God's priority was not an execution of judgment, but rather to irrefutably validate His love and truth through an open demonstration of His person; so that no accusation of any kind could ever be thrust upon His Holy Name again.

Hebrews 1:1 - God, who at sundry times and in divers manners spoke in time past unto the fathers by the prophets, 2 Has in these last days spoken unto us by His Son, whom He has appointed heir of all things, by whom also He made the worlds; 3 Who being the brightness of His glory, and the express image of His person, and upholding all things by the word of His power, when He had by Himself purged our sins, sat down on the right hand of the Majesty on high.

God's priority was not one of vengeance, nor was He anxious to retaliate against His accuser and those who had wickedly believed his lies. Rather, God's priority was to prove beyond all doubt His holy character in the hearts and minds of the faithful angels. For knowing both the rewards and risk of giving His creatures freewill, God had foreseen this inevitable rise of rebellion. For scriptures tell us, that from the very foundation of heaven and earth, God had devised a mysterious plan whereby He would forever eliminate any grounds for suspicion in the hearts of those that would believe in Him. What was God's plan? He would first "justify" Himself and THEN thoroughly avenge Himself THROUGH His heavenly host!

Ephesians 3:8 - Unto me, who am less than the least of all saints, is this grace given, that I should preach among the Gentiles the unsearchable riches of Christ; 9 And to make all men see what is the fellowship of the mystery, which from the beginning of the world has been hid in God, who created all things by Jesus Christ: 10 To the intent that now unto the principalities and powers in heavenly places might be known by the church the manifold wisdom of God, 11 According to the eternal purpose which He purposed in Christ Jesus our Lord.

I Peter 1:12 - Unto whom it was revealed, that not unto themselves [*the prophets of old*], but unto us did they minister the things, which are now reported unto you by them that have preached the gospel unto you with the Holy Ghost sent down from heaven; Which things the angels desire to look into.

Instead of immediately defending Himself, God chose to remain silent before His accuser. He did not strive to clear His name in the heavens nor win the hearts of humanity with "enticing words," He patiently waited preferring a "demonstration of His Spirit and power." Accused of being an egotist, unfair and domineering, God knew He would forever discredit all these blasphemous lies through the man Jesus Christ and the work of the cross.

I Corinthians 2:4 - And my speech and my preaching was not with enticing words of man's wisdom, but in demonstration of the Spirit and of power: 5 That your faith should not stand in the wisdom of men, but in the power of God. 6 Howbeit, we speak wisdom among them that are perfect: yet not the wisdom of this world, nor of the princes of this world, that come to naught: 7 But we speak the wisdom of God in a mystery, even the hidden wisdom, which God ordained before the world unto our glory: 8 Which none of the princes of this world knew: for had they known it, they would not have crucified the Lord of glory.

Dear reader, God delights in all His creatures and His desire is that they too would delight in Him. For that reason, He has given us His love freely and longs for our love to be freely returned; for God knows that love, if it is to be true love, MUST be freely given with absolute trust.

Satan lied and God knew it. Unfortunately, a third part of the angels didn't. Seduced by Satan's perverted and corrupt wisdom they chose his side. Theirs was a fatal choice which sadly remains an all too popular one today.

Be not deceived my friends, there is no neutral ground to take. God will not permit it. In His eyes, one's failure to stand with Him and to separate one's self from sinners is a choice to stand against Him. Consequently, as Satan's lies forced every angel to choose whom they would serve, we too are all forced to do the same. We must be separate from sinners or we too become guilty and partakers of their sins.

Matthew 12:30 - He that is not with Me is against Me; and he that gathers not with Me scatters abroad.

II John 1:9 - Whosoever transgresses, and abides not in the doctrine of Christ, has not God. He that abides in the doctrine of Christ, he has both the Father and the Son. 10 If there come any unto you, and bring not this doctrine, receive him not into your house, neither bid him God speed: 11 For he that bids him God speed is partaker of his evil deeds.

II Corinthians 6:14 - Be not unequally yoked together with unbelievers: for what fellowship has righteousness with unrighteousness, and what communion has light with darkness? 15 Or what concord has Christ with Belial? Or what part has he that believes with an infidel? 16 And what agreement has the temple of God with idols? For you are the temple of the living God; as God has said, I will dwell in them, and walk in them; and I will be their God, and they shall be My people. 17 Wherefore come out from among them, and be you separate, says the Lord, and touch not the unclean thing; and I will receive you, 18 And will be a Father unto you, and you shall be My sons and daughters, says the Lord Almighty.

Revelation 18:4 - And I heard another voice from heaven, saying, "Come out of her, My people, that you be not partakers of her sins, and that you receive not of her plagues. 5 For her sins have reached unto heaven, and God has remembered her iniquities."

FALSE ACCUSATIONS

So far, we've seen the devil deceive Eve, call God a liar, and accuse righteous Job. Are you surprised by all this? You shouldn't be. This has been Satan's manner of sin "from the beginning." And so, we were warned by Jesus that "If they have called the master of the house [*God*] Beelzebub [*Chief of Sinners*], how much more shall they call them of His household?"

I John 3:7 - Little children, let no man deceive you: he that does righteousness is righteous, even as He is righteous. 8 He that commits sin is of the devil; for the devil sinned from the beginning. For this purpose, the Son of God was manifested, that He might destroy the works of the devil.

Be not deceived, just as the righteous before us have been falsely accused by Satan and his children, so will the righteous be in our day. Let us therefore take our consolation in Christ alone.

Matthew 5:11 - Blessed are you when men shall revile you, and persecute you, and say all manner of evil against you falsely, for My sake. 12 Rejoice and be exceeding glad: for great is your reward in heaven.

False accusations have always been Satan's ammunition of choice to attack those who would choose to live godly. As a swordsman is a master of his weapon, so is our enemy with his lies.

Psalm 119:69 - The proud have forged a lie against me: but I will keep thy precepts with my whole heart.

To "forge" something is to deliberately fabricate something false in an effort to pass it off as genuine or true. Remember how at Jesus' trial they "sought false witnesses... to put Him to death, yea, though many false witnesses came, yet they found none?" The problem wasn't a shortage of accusations. The problem was the credibility of the witnesses. They were unable to "forge" a lie against our Lord and Savior. Then came two false witnesses which said, "This fellow said, I am able to destroy the temple of God and build it again in three days." However, what Jesus really said was, "Destroy this temple [*His body*], and in three days I will raise it up." How skillful the adversary is in twisting the words of God.

The Bible contains many such accounts of God's faithful being not only falsely accused, but aggressively as well. We see Stephen accused of speaking "blasphemous words against Moses, and against God." In Macedonia, Paul and Silas were accused of troubling a whole city, beaten and cast into prison! In Thessalonica their preaching caused such an uproar that they were actually accused of "turning the world upside down!"

Acts 6:8 - And Stephen, full of faith and power, did great wonders and miracles among the people... 10 And they were not able to resist the wisdom and the spirit by which he spoke. 11 Then they suborned men, which said, "We have heard him speak blasphemous words against Moses, and against God." 12 And they stirred up the people, and the elders, and the scribes, and came upon him, and caught him, and brought him to the council, 13 And set up false witnesses, which said, "This man ceases not to speak blasphemous words against this holy place, and the law: 14 For we have heard him say, that this Jesus of Nazareth shall destroy this place, and shall change the customs which Moses delivered us." 15 And all that sat in the council, looking steadfastly on him, saw his face as it had been the face of an angel.

Acts 16:19 - ...they caught Paul and Silas, and drew them into the marketplace unto the rulers, 20 And brought them to the magistrates, saying, "These men being Jews do exceedingly trouble our city, 21 For they teach customs which are not lawful for us to receive, neither to observe we being Romans."

Acts 17:4 - And of them believed and consorted with Paul and Silas; and of the devout Greeks a great multitude, and of the chief women not a few. 5 But the Jews which believed not moved with envy, took unto them certain lewd fellows of the baser sort, and gathered a company, and set all the city on an uproar, and assaulted the house of Jason, and sought to bring them out to the people. 6 And when they found them not, they drew Jason and certain brethren unto the rulers of the city, crying, "These that have turned the world upside down are come hither also; 7 Whom Jason has received: and these all do contrary to the decrees of Caesar, saying that there is another king, one Jesus."

Afterwards Paul was called "a pestilent fellow, a mover of sedition among all the Jews of the world, a ringleader of the sect of the Nazarenes: who has gone about and profaned the temple," (Acts 24:5). Even before Festus, the governor of Judea, the Jews persecution persisted as they "laid many grievous complaints against Paul, which they could not prove," (Acts 25:7, 8).

The devil and his "children" will never cease forging their lies against the church. Therefore, you should not be surprised when they begin to attack you too.

II Timothy 3:8 - Now as Jannes and Jambres withstood Moses, so do these also resist the truth: men of corrupt minds, reprobate concerning the faith. 9 But they shall proceed no further: for their folly shall be manifest unto all men, as theirs also was. 10 But you have fully known my doctrine, manner of life, purpose, faith, longsuffering, charity, patience, 11 Persecutions, afflictions, which came unto me at Antioch, at Iconium, at Lystra; what persecutions I endured: but out of them all the Lord delivered me. 12 Yea, and all that will live godly in Christ Jesus shall suffer persecution.

MADE A LITTLE LOWER THAN THE ANGELS

Hebrews 2:9 - But we see Jesus, who was made a little lower than the angels for the suffering of death, crowned with glory and honor; that He by the grace of God should taste death for every man. 10 For it became Him, for Whom are all things, and by Whom are all things, in bringing many sons unto glory, to make the Captain of their salvation perfect through sufferings. 11 For both He that sanctifies and they who are sanctified are all of one: for which cause He is not ashamed to call them brethren... 14 For as much then as the children are partakers of flesh and blood, He also Himself likewise took part of the same; that through death He might destroy Him that had the power of death, that is, the devil; 15 And deliver them who through fear of death were all their lifetime subject to bondage.

Now many perceive Satan's "power of death" in verse 14 to be the same as having the "keys of death" in Revelation 1:18. It's not, for in Psalm 68:20 it shows that "our God is the God of salvation; and unto God belong the issues of death." The devil has never had the unilateral power to take life. God alone determines and permits the time of every man's death, not the devil. We see this proven in the Old Testament where the dead were brought back to life by God's servants.

I Kings 17:18 - And she said unto Elijah, "What have I to do with you, O man of God? Are you come unto me to call my sin to remembrance, and to slay my son?" 19 And he said unto her, "Give me your son." And he took him out of her bosom, and carried him up into a loft, where he abode, and laid him upon his own bed. 20 And he cried unto the LORD, and said, "O LORD my God, Have You also brought evil upon the widow with whom I sojourn, by slaying her son?" 21 And he stretched himself upon the child three times, and cried unto the LORD, and said, "O LORD my God, I pray You, let this child's soul come into him again." 22 And the LORD heard the voice of Elijah; and the soul of the child came into him again, and he revived. 23 And Elijah took the child and brought him down out of the chamber into the house and delivered him unto his mother: and Elijah said, "See, your son lives". 24 And the woman said to Elijah, "Now by this I know that you are a man of God, and that the word of the LORD in your mouth is truth."

II Kings 4:32 - And when Elisha was come into the house, behold, the child was dead, and laid upon his bed. 33 He went in therefore, and shut the door upon them both, and prayed unto the LORD. 34 And he went up, and lay upon the child, and put his mouth upon his mouth, and his eyes upon his eyes, and his hands upon his hands: and he stretched himself upon the child; and the flesh of the child waxed warm. 35 Then he returned and walked in the house to and fro; and went up and stretched himself upon him: and the child sneezed seven times, and the child opened his eyes.

II Kings 13:20 - And Elisha died, and they buried him. And the bands of the Moabites invaded the land at the coming in of the year. 21 And it came to pass, as they were burying a man, that, behold, they spied a band of men; and they cast the man into the sepulcher of Elisha: and when the man was let down, and touched the bones of Elisha, he revived, and stood up on his feet.

In the New Testament we see that not only did Jesus raise Lazarus, the daughter of Jairus who was one of the rulers of the synagogue, and the widow's son from the dead, He also gave to His disciples the "power to raise the dead" even prior to His death on the cross. For the power of life and death are God's alone, for as we saw that the devil could never have killed Job's family if God had not permitted it. Likewise, concerning the "beast" of Revelation "it [*permission*] was given him to make war with the saints and to overcome [*kill*] them," (Revelation 13:7).

That is not to deny that there are certain things people can do that may indeed affect God's determination in the time of their death. Some examples would be eating properly and exercising versus food, alcohol, and substance abuse, as well as suicide. However, without God's permissiveness, death cannot comply any man's desire to die.

Revelation 9:6 - And in those days shall men seek death and shall not find it; and shall desire to die, and death shall flee from them.

Proverbs 18:21 states, "Death and life are in the power of the tongue," and this is where the devil's "power of death" rests. All he can do on his own is lie, undermine, distort, and pervert the truth of God, and so he intentionally mishandles it by overly emphasizing certain parts while minimizing or even outright ignoring other indispensable parts. This is known as the "Strain at a gnat and swallow a camel" religion of hypocrites.

Matthew 23:23 - Woe unto you, scribes and Pharisees, hypocrites! for you pay tithes of mint and anise and cumin, and have omitted the weightier matters of the law, judgment, mercy, and faith: these ought you to have done, and not to leave the other undone. 24 You blind guides, which strain at a gnat, and swallow a camel. 25 Woe unto you, scribes and Pharisees, hypocrites! for you make clean the outside of the cup and of the platter, but within they are full of extortion and excess. 26 You blind Pharisees, cleanse first that which is within the cup and platter, that the outside of them may be clean also.

The result of this kind of religion is death, because not only does it fail to reconcile men to God; it leads them away from the truth that is meant to set them free. Thus, it is Satan's strategy to try and shipwreck every Christian's faith with false "doctrines of devils" and hypocrisy or to utterly discourage them with an endless flood of false accusations and persecutions.

I Timothy 1:18 - This charge I commit unto you my son Timothy, according to the prophecies which went before on you, that by them you might war a good warfare; 19 Holding faith, and a good conscience; which some having put away concerning faith have made shipwreck.

I Timothy 4:1 - Now the Spirit speaks expressly, that in the latter times some shall depart from the faith, giving heed to seducing spirits, and doctrines of devils; 2 Speaking lies in hypocrisy; having their conscience seared with a hot iron.

To counter the devil's crusade of deception, the Holy Spirit has been given to illuminate the heart of the yielded believer to God's precious truths. Not just the written truth, but the Living Truth Himself! God came in the flesh to discredit Satan's lies and has long since returned via His Holy Spirit to establish true faith in the heart of every believer that the divine nature of Christ might be fully formed in them.

Galatians 4:19 - My little children, of whom I travail in birth again until Christ be formed in you.

Ephesians 4:13 - Till we all come in the unity of the faith, and of the knowledge of the Son of God, unto a perfect man, unto the measure of the stature of the fulness of Christ: 14 That we henceforth be no more children, tossed to and fro, and carried about with every wind of doctrine, by the sleight of men, and cunning craftiness, whereby they lie in wait to deceive; 15 But speaking the truth in love, may grow up into Him in all things, which is the head, even Christ

II Thessalonians 2:13 - But we are bound to give thanks always to God for you, brethren beloved of the Lord, because God has from the beginning chosen you to salvation through sanctification of the Spirit and belief of the truth: 14 Whereunto He called you by our gospel, to the obtaining of the glory of our Lord Jesus Christ.

II Peter 1:3 - According as His divine power has given unto us all things that pertain unto life and godliness, through the knowledge of Him that has called us to glory and virtue: 4 Whereby are given unto us exceeding great and precious promises: that by these you might be partakers of the divine nature, having escaped the corruption that is in the world through lust.

DISPROVING SATAN'S LIES

I John 3:8 - He that commits sin is of the devil; for the devil sinned from the beginning. For this purpose, the Son of God was manifested, that He might destroy the works of the devil.

Philippians 2:5 - Let this mind be in you, which was also in Christ Jesus: 6 Who, being in the form of God, thought it not robbery to be equal with God: 7 But made Himself of no reputation, and took upon Him the form of a servant, and was made in the likeness of men: 8 And being found in fashion as a man, He humbled Himself, and became obedient unto death, even the death of the cross. 9 Wherefore God also has highly exalted Him and given Him a name which is above every name: 10 That at the name of Jesus every knee should bow, of things in heaven, and things in earth, and things under the earth; 11 And that every tongue should confess that Jesus Christ is Lord, to the glory of God the Father.

Yes, the Supreme Governor of the universe made Himself lower than the angels. In that earthen vessel of flesh and blood of the man Jesus Christ dwelt "all the fullness of the Godhead bodily." It was there in that frail, humble form of humanity that the revelation of God's eternal glory was unveiled and through it His divine character was clearly and undeniably revealed to all.

Colossians 1:12 - Giving thanks unto the Father, which has made us meet to be partakers of the inheritance of the saints in light: 13 Who has delivered us from the power of darkness, and has translated us into the kingdom of His dear Son: 14 In whom we have redemption through His blood, even the forgiveness of sins: 15 Who is the image of the invisible God, the firstborn of every creature: 16 For by Him were all things created, that are in heaven, and that are in earth, visible and invisible, whether they be thrones, or dominions, or principalities, or powers: all things were created by Him, and for Him: 17 And He is before all things, and by Him all things consist. 18 And He is the head of the body, the church: who is the beginning, the firstborn from the dead; that in all things He might have the preeminence. 19 For it pleased the Father that in Him should all fulness dwell; 20 And, having made peace through the blood of His cross, by Him to reconcile all things unto Himself; by Him, I say, whether they be things in earth, or things in heaven.

Colossians 2:9 - For in Him dwells all the fulness of the Godhead bodily.

Isaiah 52:10 - The LORD made bare [*revealed*] His Holy Arm in the eyes of all the nations; and all the ends of the earth shall see the salvation of our God.

Yes, He who was once "sitting upon a throne, high and lifted up" descended from heaven to take upon Himself the lowly form of a man for all the nations to see. Yet do we truly believe this?

Isaiah 53:1 - Who has believed our report? and to whom is the arm of the LORD revealed? 2 For He shall grow up before Him as a tender plant, and as a root out of a dry ground: He has no form nor comeliness; and when we shall see Him, there is no beauty that we should desire Him.

John 12:41 - These things said Esaias, when he saw His glory, and spoke of Him.

Think about that for a minute, "a tender plant... a root out of dry ground?" What does that really mean?

Let's suppose there are two containers, in each you plant identical tomato seedlings. The first container you water every other day as is recommended, the other you sporadically water once or twice a week. The first grows as it should, strong and healthy and becomes a hardy looking tomato plant.

The other however which you watered once or twice a week, grows, but having its roots in dry soil remains a frail and tender plant. When the two are compared side by side, the favor goes immediately to the robust plant, as the second one has no real visible potentials to compel you to choose it over the other. This my friends is the biblical record of the incarnation of Christ.

Isaiah 53:2 - For He shall grow up before Him as a tender plant, and as a root out of a dry ground: He has no form nor comeliness; and when we shall see Him, there is no beauty that we should desire Him.

He who once descended upon Mount Sinai with thunders, lightning, and fire with a thick cloud of darkness, causing the whole mount to quake greatly, the same came into the world as a lowly infant destined to grow up and become the pinnacle point of all eternity for every living creature.

Luke 2:34 - And Simeon blessed them, and said unto Mary his mother, Behold, this child is set for the fall and rising again of many in Israel; and for a sign which shall be spoken against.

The Almighty did not come with an appearance like that of King Saul, who was obviously a "choice young man" and "goodly [*handsome*] and there was not a goodlier person than he: from his shoulders upward he was higher than any of the people," (I Samuel 9:2). For surely this was the kind of Christ many were looking for, and still are. But no, God took for Himself a body with "no form nor comeliness" that "when we shall see Him, there is no beauty that we should desire Him."

God did not attempt to prove He was worthy of both men and angels' loyalty and love by Jesus coming into the world with a majestic appearance, unmatched beauty, and an intimidating display of power. No, instead, having laid all that aside, it was in a beaten, whipped, spat upon, crucified and pierced body, that He silently, yet openly, undeniably proved His love for us and forever settled any question of His being worthy of all glory, honor and power.

God repudiated the lies of the devil by humbly taking a form lower than the angels' and was literally birthed into the world He had made through the womb of a virgin as a child. As such, He lived a humble and godly life that would forever prove to both the angels and humanity that He was worthy of all the love and service of His creatures. As a man, Jesus by example showed men how they ought to live their lives; as everything that Jesus said and did was in full accordance with the will of His Father.

John 4:34 - Jesus says unto them, "My meat is to do the will of Him that sent Me, and to finish His work."

John 5:19 - Then answered Jesus and said unto them, "Verily, verily, I say unto you, The Son [*in His humanity*] can do nothing of

Himself, but what He sees the Father do: for what things so ever He does, these also do the Son likewise."

Having Himself fully experienced the benefit of obedience by the things He suffered; Jesus set the standard for all who would thereafter choose to live godly.

Philippians 2:8 - And being found in fashion as a man, He humbled Himself, and became obedient unto death, even the death of the cross.

Hebrew 5:8 - Though He were a Son, He still learned obedience by the things which He suffered; 9 And being made perfect, He became the author of eternal salvation unto all them that obey Him.

I Peter 2:21 - For even hereunto were you called: because Christ also suffered for us, leaving us an example, that you should follow His steps: 22 Who did no sin, neither was guile found in His mouth: 23 Who, when He was reviled, reviled not again; when He suffered, He threatened not; but committed Himself to Him that judges righteously: 24 Who His own self bare our sins in His own body on the tree, that we, being dead to sins, should live unto righteousness: by whose stripes you were healed.

GOD WILL PROVIDE HIMSELF A LAMB

One of the greatest biblical examples in the Old Testament of God giving His only begotten Son for the world is seen in Abraham offering up Isaac as a burnt offering. For in it Abraham understood that in Isaac was the promise of the inheritance. Thus, if God was requiring Isaac to be slain and consumed in the flames of the burnt offering, Abraham knew God would have to raise Isaac from the dead again.

Hebrew 11:17 - By faith Abraham, when he was tried, offered up Isaac: and he that had received the promises offered up his only begotten son, 18 Of whom it was said, "That in Isaac shall your seed be called." 19 Accounting that God was able to raise him up, even from the dead; from whence also he received him in a figure.

Having been instructed by God to offer up Isaac as a burnt offering, Abraham arose early and with the help of his son Isaac and two young men the animals were made ready and loaded with the wood for the burnt offering. Then they all traveled three days to the place where God had directed Abraham. Upon their arrival, Abraham instructed the young men to wait while Isaac and he went to "worship God." Here was the father of faith knowing the hardest task of his life was before him, and he called it "worshipping God." Nevertheless, Abraham went forth fully resolved to obey God and was committed to his slaying of Isaac and placing his body upon the altar to be consumed as a burnt offering unto God. Even so, he turned to those two young men with him and in faith assured them that Isaac and himself would both return again.

Genesis 22:6 - And Abraham took the wood of the burnt offering and laid it upon Isaac his son; and he took the fire in his hand, and a knife; and they went both of them together. 7 And Isaac spoke unto Abraham his father, and said, "My father," and he said, "Here am I, my son." And he said, "Behold the fire and the wood: but where is the lamb for a burnt offering?" 8 And Abraham said, "My son, God will provide Himself a lamb for a burnt offering." So, they went both of them together.

And there in verse eight above we see the Spirit of Prophecy resting upon Abraham and bringing forth the testimony of Jesus Christ; for Abraham tells Isaac that "God will provide Himself a lamb for a burnt offering."

But not only did God provide a lamb for Isaac's immediate redemption, in truth He provided Himself as that Lamb which alone could take away the sin of the world. For the Almighty God "was brought as a lamb to the slaughter" as our "offering for sin." He who is the giver of all life "poured out His soul unto death." He who is our Judge, our Lawgiver, and our King, allowed Himself to be numbered with the transgressors," (Isaiah the entire 53rd chapter).

Philippians 2:9 - Wherefore God also has highly exalted Him and given Him a name which is above every name: 10 That at the name of Jesus every knee should bow, of things in heaven, and things in earth, and things under the earth; 11 And that every tongue should confess that Jesus Christ is Lord, to the glory of God the Father.

By the cross it was proven that Satan had lied! Jesus "spoiled principalities and powers, He made a show of them openly, triumphing over them in it," (Colossians 2:15). God was not merely doing what He wanted or considered most pleasant for Himself. Rather, as a loving Creator and Father, He did what was best for those He had created knowing full well the cost that had to be paid.

Luke 22:41 - And He was withdrawn from them about a stone's cast, and kneeled down, and prayed, 42 Saying, "Father, if You be willing, remove this cup from Me: nevertheless, not My will, but Your will be done." 43 And there appeared an angel unto Him from heaven, strengthening Him. 44 And being in an agony He prayed more earnestly: and His sweat was as it were great drops of blood falling down to the ground.

Romans 15:3 - For even Christ pleased not Himself; but, as it is written, "The reproaches of them that reproached You fell on Me."

John 5:30 - I can of Mine own self do nothing: as I hear, I judge: and My judgment is just; because I seek not Mine own will, but the will of the Father which has sent Me.

Hebrews 5:7 - Who in the days of His flesh, when He had offered up prayers and supplications with strong crying and tears unto Him that was able to save Him from death and was heard in that He feared; 8 Though He were a Son, yet learned He obedience by the things which He suffered; 9 And being made perfect, He became the author of eternal salvation unto all them that obey Him.

The Almighty God did not come as an overbearing and self-serving master. No, He came as a lowly, yet loving Shepherd seeking those that were lost, and willing to lead all who would follow Him in paths of righteousness to the restoration of their souls. If all this has not been sufficient to clear His glorious name, then consider the words of Jesus below.

Revelation 3:18 - I counsel you to buy of Me gold tried in the fire, that you may be rich; and white raiment, that you may be clothed, and that the shame of your nakedness does not appear; and anoint your eyes with eye salve, that you might see. 19 As many as I love, I rebuke and chasten: be zealous therefore, and repent. 20 Behold, I stand at the door, and knock: if any man hears My voice, and open the door, I will come in to him, and will sup with him, and he with Me. 21 To him that overcomes will I grant to sit with Me in my throne, even as I also overcame, and am set down with My Father in His throne. 22 He that has an ear, let him hear what the Spirit says unto the churches.

What do all these passages of scripture affirm? What does the birth, life, death and resurrection of Jesus Christ prove? It proves God is not egotistical.

It proves God is not self-centered! It proves God is both just and merciful! It proves God is a patient, loving and responsible Creator! Furthermore, it undeniably proves God is not only willing, but desirous to share His throne!

II Timothy 2:11 - It is a faithful saying: "If we be dead with Him, we shall also live with Him 12 If we suffer with Him, we shall also reign with Him. But if we deny Him, He also will deny us."

Romans 8:16 - The Spirit itself bears witness with our spirit, that we are the children of God. 17 And if we are His children, then we are heirs, even heirs of God, for we are joint-heirs with Christ. For if so be that we suffer with Him, that we may be also glorified together. 18 For I reckon that the sufferings of this present time are not worthy to be compared with that glory which shall be revealed in us.

So much for all those blasphemous lies of the devil. For by God being manifested in the flesh, the devil was openly condemned and proven a seditious liar! In light of both history and scripture, God forever has proven Himself the meekest, most thoughtful, merciful, and generous of all living beings! Praise be to the glorious name of Jesus!

LIGHTNING FALLING FROM HEAVEN

Luke 10:17 - And the seventy returned again with joy, saying, "Lord, even the devils are subject unto us through Your name." 18 And He said unto them, "I beheld Satan as lightning fall from heaven."

The above verse is a very enlightening piece of scripture. By it we learn that while the disciples were away, Jesus (who was in prayer and fasting often), "beheld Satan as lightning fall from heaven." Now some people think Jesus literally saw Satan cast to the earth. Others believe Jesus saw this in a metaphorical sense, as a spiritual result of the seventy's mission. However, neither of these views have any other scriptural support apart from this passage.

A third opinion is that Jesus did indeed have a vision, but it was prophetic; meaning the event He witnessed was yet to take place. It is this view which has the most support of the scriptures. Personally, I believe it was this vision which enabled Jesus to set His face like flint toward the cross.

Isaiah 50:7 - For the Lord GOD will help Me; therefore, shall I not be confounded: therefore, have I set My face like a flint, and I know that I shall not be ashamed. 8 He is near that justifies Me; who will contend with Me? let us stand together: who is Mine adversary? let him come near to Me. 9 Behold, the Lord GOD will help Me; who is he that shall condemn Me? Lo, they all shall wax old as a garment; the moth shall eat them up.

According to scripture, Jesus "beheld Satan... fall," past tense. Now admittingly, in prophetic visions it is normal to see events come to pass before the events literally happen. The books of Isaiah, Daniel, and Revelation should provide adequate proof for any skeptic of that being so. However, the most significant proof I find that this was a "prophetic vision" and not just an "event" resulting from the disciple's mission comes from other statements made later on by Jesus Himself.

John 12:23 - And Jesus answered them, saying, "The hour is come, that the Son of man should be glorified. 24 Verily, verily, I say unto you, except a corn of wheat fall into the ground and die, it abides alone: but if it die, it will bring forth much fruit... 27 Now is My soul troubled; and what shall I say? Father, save Me from this hour: but for this cause came I unto this hour. 28 Father, glorify Your name." Then came there a voice from heaven, saying, "I have both glorified it, and will glorify it again." 29 The people therefore, that stood by, and heard it, said that it thundered: others said, "An angel spoke to Him." 30 Jesus answered and said, "This voice came not because of Me, but for your sakes. 31 **Now is the judgment of this world. Now shall the prince of this world be cast out**. 32 And I, if I be lifted up from the earth, will draw all men unto Me." 33 This he said, signifying what death He should die. 34 The people answered Him, "We have heard out of the law that Christ abides forever: and how then do you say, "The Son of man must be lifted up? who is this Son of man?"

John 14:28 - You have heard how I said unto you, I go away and come again unto you. If you love Me, you would rejoice, because I said I go unto My Father: for My Father [*being omnipresent*] is greater than I [*as a man*]. 29 And now I told you before it come to pass, that when it is come to pass, you might believe. 30 Hereafter I will not talk much with you: for **the prince of this world is coming**, and has nothing in Me.

John 16:7 - I tell you the truth; it is expedient for you that I go away: for if I [*as a man*] go not away, the Comforter will not come unto you. But if I depart, I will send Him unto you. 8 And when He is come, He will reprove the world of sin, and of righteousness, and of judgment... 11 Of judgment because **the prince of this world is judged**.

In these verses Jesus referred to Satan's fall as something about to happen, and He also stated that "the prince of this world is judged." Again, spoken in the past-tense. Note also, that it is just prior to His crucifixion that Jesus told those with Him that "NOW shall the prince of this world be cast out," and then He further warned them that "the prince of this world is coming." It should be evident to the reader that in these scriptures Jesus was announcing that day to the people with Him that these events were about to occur, and not afar off in the future.

The time of occurrence appears to be linked with the time of Christ's death, or as John 12:23 refers to it, the time for Jesus to be "glorified." Jesus knew the devil "has nothing in Me" for while He was locked in time and space by His humanity, He remained in constant subjection to His Holy Infinite Spirit. Having successfully lived as a man not governed by His flesh, it was impossible for the devil to find any place to justly accuse Him. Jesus' secret? He committed Himself to the Spirit and kept His eyes on the joy set before Him.

Four key words to remember: "Justified, glorified, judged" and "condemned." God was "justified" and therefore "glorified." The devil was "judged" and therefore "condemned," both at the same time. Both by the same event; the shedding of God's blood on Calvary!

WAR IN HEAVEN

Revelation 12:5 - And she brought forth a man child, who was to rule all nations with a rod of iron: and her child was caught up unto God, and to His throne... 7 And there was war in heaven: Michael and his angels fought against the dragon; and the dragon fought and his angels, 8 And prevailed not; neither was their place found any more in heaven. 9 And the great dragon was cast out, that old serpent, called the Devil, and Satan, which deceives the whole world: he was cast out into the earth, and his angels were cast out with him. 10 And I heard a loud voice saying in heaven, "Now is come salvation, and strength, and the kingdom of our God, and the power of His Christ: for the accuser of our brethren is cast down, which accused them before our God day and night." 11 And they overcame him by the blood of the Lamb, and by the word of their testimony; and they loved not their lives unto the death. 12 Therefore, rejoice you heavens and you that dwell in them.

Here we are told of an awesome war which occurred in heaven, a war which many believe has yet to take place. But in light of what we have heard from the words of Jesus prior to His going to the cross and this passage in Revelation, "her child was caught up unto God, and to His throne... And there was war in heaven," it seems evident this war occurred either at Christ's death on the cross, His resurrection, or perhaps as late as the time of His ascension. However, I am persuaded it was most probably at the time of His completed work on the cross when He stated, "It is finished."

John 19:28 - ...Jesus **knowing that all things were now accomplished**, that the scripture might be fulfilled, said, "I thirst." 29 Now there was set a vessel full of vinegar and they filled a sponge with vinegar, put it upon hyssop, and put it to His mouth. 30 When Jesus therefore had received the vinegar, He said, "**It is finished**," and bowed his head and gave up the ghost.

Colossians 2:13 - And you, being dead in your sins and the uncircumcision of your flesh, has He quickened together with Him, having forgiven you all trespasses. 14 Blotting out the handwriting of ordinances that was against us, which was contrary to us, and took it out of the way, nailing it to His cross, 15 having spoiled principalities and powers, **He made a show of them openly and triumphed over them in it** [*the cross*].

Now remember, Jesus began His ministry with the miracle of turning water into wine at a wedding which He and His disciples were invited to. For there were six vessels of stone which held water at this wedding which was there solely because the Jews had their vain religious tradition whereby they would not eat unless they had washed their hands. It was this very water that Jesus used and turned into wine, and it was "good wine."

In doing so, by having replaced the water with wine, Jesus had literally removed this vain work of purification from the wedding and replaced it with what would become symbolic to His followers of that which alone could purify men from their sins, His blood. (And never forget, it is still all about The Wedding.) Yet here at the end of His earthly ministry we see men giving to Him vinegar to drink just before He says, "It is finished." But do you not know that the consequence of neglected wine is that it turns to vinegar? Thus, their actions were a testimony against them, that they wanted nothing to do with Jesus or His Gospel. As Isaiah foretold, He was despised and rejected of men and considered accursed of God by them.

But through it all, the faithful angels having "seen" the life and death of Christ were now fully persuaded that God was deserving of all their love and service. United and energized, they fought against Satan and forever expelled him and his angels from heaven. Yet, not only did the holy angels fight for God, they fought for God's people as well; and they continue to minister to the saints according to God's will. Satan can no longer come before the throne of God and hurl his blasphemous accusations. He and his lies had been put to an open shame at the cross, (Colossians 2:14, 15). God's victory could not be hidden or denied. For by this pinnacle event of all eternity, God "made peace through the blood of His cross... to reconcile all things unto Himself; by Him I say, whether they be things in earth, or things in heaven," (Colossians 2:12-20).

But what does God's word say now to those on earth? "WOE to the inhabitants of the earth... for the devil is come unto you having great wrath for he knows that he has but a short time," (Revelation

12:12). Having been exposed and humiliated by his defeat, Satan knows that his days are numbered. Therefore, he seeks to do as much damage through his deceit as he continues to "cast out of his mouth water as a flood [*false teachings*] after the woman [*church*], that he might cause her to be carried away of the flood," (Rev. 12:16). This is evident in the Apostle Paul's statement to the Galatians, "I marvel that you are so soon removed [*carried away*] from Him that called you into the grace of Christ unto another Gospel: which is not another; but there be some that trouble you and would pervert the Gospel of Christ. But though we, or an angel from heaven, preach any other Gospel unto you than that you have received, let him be accursed," (1:6-8).

The devil has a foaming hatred and wrath towards all humanity, but especially so against Israel and the Church. Basically, because men are created in the image of God and He proved His love for man via the work of the cross. Therefore, the devil's only avenue of vengeance toward God is his constant cunning pursuit for any opportunity to turn man against man in hatred for each other as he attempts to deceive, persecute, and destroy the Body of Christ. He knows he can't defeat God, for he was literally cast out of heaven and knows his time is short. Therefore, ever since then his wrath has been constantly demonstrated against the church and Israel as his only means of retaliation against God.

But never let us succumb to fearing this fallen adversary, rather let us trust and fear God and give Him all glory. For just as there was no uncertainty among the heavenly angels, neither should there be among the people of God. Otherwise, as the devil and his angels were cast out for their sins and unbelief, we too receive similar condemnation.

Hebrews 4:1 - Let us therefore fear, lest, a promise being left us of entering into His rest, any of you should seem to come short of it. 2 For unto us was the gospel preached, as well as unto them. But the word preached did not profit them because it was not mixed with faith in them that heard it.

Rather, just as the holy angels fought whole heartedly for God and overcame him by witnessing the shed blood of the Lamb and hearing the word of His testimony, so let us too. Be brave, be strong, have faith and live like saints of the living God!

I Corinthians 16:13 - Watch you and stand fast in the faith, quit you like men, be strong.

Hebrews 12:12 - Wherefore lift up the hands which hang down, and the feeble knees; 13 And make straight paths for your feet, lest that which is lame be turned out of the way; but rather let it be healed. 14 Follow peace with all men, and holiness, without which no man shall see the Lord. 15 Looking diligently lest any man fail of the grace of God an any root of bitterness springing up trouble you, and many thereby are defiled.

Since the fall of the once anointed cherub Lucifer, "the kingdom of heaven suffers violence, and the violent [or, *the aggressive must*] take it by force" for the devil will oppose to the end all who would strive to enter in, (Matthew 11:12). Never forget, just as the angels and saints of old overcame, so can every true believer today!

It is to our shame that it is so hard for us to endure momentary hardships and to resist our temptations. Especially when God has promised no temptation would be so great that we could not overcome it, nor will He fail to give us a way to escape it. We should esteem the "reproaches of Christ greater riches" than all the riches of the world. We should rejoice and count it all joy when we are considered worthy to suffer for His name. But do we?

Romans 8:18 - For I reckon that the sufferings of this present time are not worthy to be compared with the glory which shall be revealed in us.

Come on saints! Let's pick up our crosses and follow Him. Unlike Jesus, we deserve our crosses. For without Him your cross would be only your just reward and shame. But now, even today, it can be a witness of your love and a testimony to His glory! Set your heart to do that which He has promised you can and must do, and "overcome the wicked one by the blood of the Lamb" and the word of your testimony. Pick up your cross and follow Him! For worthy is the Lamb which was slain to receive glory and honor and power!

1 John 5:20 - And we know that the Son of God is come, and has given us an understanding, that we may know Him that is true, and we are in Him that is true, even in His Son Jesus Christ. This is the true God, and eternal life.

Live for Jesus Christ the King!
For it will make it easier for you to die for Him!

<u>Grace</u>

Grace, and yes, it is amazing grace. But do you really understand it? Because, if you fail to understand the purpose and workings of God's grace, then it is almost certain you will fall short of allowing it to accomplish in your life all that God intended it to. I know if you are reading this book, then surely you have heard it before that "by grace you are saved," but have you not also heard God's lamenting cry that, "My people perish for lack of knowledge?"

It is only by grace that we could even hope to have ears to hear the wisdom that the Spirit is trying to speak to God's people. Nevertheless, we still need to be listening and willing to respond to whatever the Holy Spirit is instructing us to *do* if we are to have a realistic hope to escape the wrath to come. For never forget, while admonitions were given to all the saints in the Seven Churches of Revelation, it was only to the "overcomers" that had "ears to hear" that Jesus spoke all those wonderful promises.

Luke 21:36 - Watch you therefore, and pray always, that you may be accounted worthy to escape all these things that shall come to pass, and to stand before the Son of man.

Hebrews 12:25 - See that you refuse not Him that speaks. For if they escaped not who refused Him that spoke on earth, much more shall we not escape if we turn away from Him that speaks from heaven: 26 Whose voice then shook the earth: but now He has promised, saying, "Yet once more I shake not the earth only, but also heaven." 27 And this word, "Yet once more," signifies the removing of those things that are shaken, as of things that are made, that those things which cannot be shaken may remain. 28 Wherefore we receiving a kingdom which cannot be moved, let us have grace, whereby we may serve God acceptably with reverence *and* godly fear.

Revelation 15:2 - And I saw as it were a sea of glass mingled with fire: and them that had gotten the victory over the beast, and over his image, and over his mark, and over the number of his name, stand on the sea of glass, having the harps of God.

The following list contains three things that God's word teaches us fundamentally about His grace. Not only are these truths plainly asserted in scriptures, biblical history repeatedly affirms these fundamental truths without partiality as it records both the triumphs and failures of those who professed to believe in God.

1. Grace is sufficient.
2. Grace can be frustrated.
3. Grace can be received in vain.

First, regarding grace's sufficiency in the life of the believer, Paul was assured by God that whatever temptations he might encounter, as well as the trials and persecutions he must suffer for the cause of Christ, he had this consolation whereby he could be comforted; His grace would always be adequate to see Paul through it all to the glory of His name.

II Corinthians 1:3 - Blessed be God, even the Father of our Lord Jesus Christ, the Father of mercies, and the God of all comfort; 4 Who comforts us in all our tribulation, that we may be able to comfort them which are in any trouble, by the comfort wherewith we ourselves are comforted of God. 5 For as the sufferings of Christ abound in us, so our consolation also abounds by Christ. 6 And whether we be afflicted, it is for your consolation and salvation, which is effectual in the enduring of the same sufferings which we also suffer: or whether we be comforted, it is for your consolation and salvation. 7 And our hope of you is steadfast, knowing, that as you are partakers of the sufferings, so shall you be also of the consolation.

Colossians 1:23 - If you continue in the faith grounded and settled, and be not moved away from the hope of the gospel, which you have heard, and which was preached to every creature which is under heaven; whereof I Paul am made a minister; 24 Who now rejoice in my sufferings for you, and fill up that which is behind of the afflictions of Christ in my flesh for His body's sake, which is the church: 25 Whereof I am made a minister, according to the dispensation of God which is given to me for you, to fulfil the word of God; 26 Even the mystery which has been hid from ages and from generations, but now is made manifest to His saints: 27 To whom God would make known what is the riches of the glory of this mystery among the Gentiles; which is Christ in you, the hope of glory.

Through everything Paul had to endure, God was teaching him that his confidence must only be placed in His wisdom and grace. And yet, it was when Paul was brought face to face with his own frailty and limitations that he experienced God's fullness in a way he never could in all those other areas where his own strength or wisdom was found to be adequate, such as in his making and mending tents.

II Corinthians 12:9 - And He said unto me, "My grace is sufficient for you: for My strength is made perfect in weakness." Most gladly therefore will I rather glory in my infirmities, that the power of Christ may rest upon me.

But when it came to the things that pertain to salvation; doing the work of the ministry, fighting the good fight of faith, or running the race, Paul knew full well he could not do those things apart from the grace of God given unto him.

I Timothy 1:11 - According to the glorious gospel of the blessed God, which was committed to my trust. 12 And I thank Christ Jesus our Lord, who has enabled me, for that He counted me faithful, putting me into the ministry.

Furthermore, the fact that God had given such empowering grace unto him, Paul was fully aware that he needed to take full advantage of it if he was to succeed in completing the work that God was requiring him to do.

I Corinthians 9:16 - For though I preach the gospel, I have nothing to glory of. For its necessity has been placed upon me. Yea, woe unto me if I preach not the gospel!

II Timothy 4:6 - For I am now ready to be offered, and the time of my departure is at hand. 7 I have fought a good fight, I have finished my course, I have kept the faith: 8 Henceforth there is laid up for me a crown of righteousness, which the Lord, the Righteous Judge, shall give me at that day: and not to me only, but unto all them also that love His appearing.

Yet, though this grace was freely given to Paul, and could never be earned by him, he knew it could not work for him, in him, and through him, unless he surrendered himself completely into God's hands.

Matthew 16:24 - Then said Jesus unto His disciples, If any man will come after Me, let him deny himself, and take up his cross, and follow Me. 25 For whosoever will save his life shall lose it: and whosoever will lose his life for My sake shall find it.

Hebrews 10:31 - It is a fearful thing to fall into the hands of the living God.

Paul understood the necessity of being crucified with Christ if he was going to have the life of Christ live in and through him. He knew "the faith of the Son of God" was given unto him so that he might be empowered to wholly give himself unto God and complete the work which God had assigned unto him, and thereby glorify the name of Jesus Christ.

Galatians 2:20 - I am crucified with Christ: nevertheless, I live; yet not I, but Christ lives in me: and the life which I now live in the flesh I live by the faith of the Son of God, who loved me, and gave Himself for me. 21 I do not frustrate the grace of God: for if righteousness come by the law, then Christ is dead in vain.

God's desire for His people was never satisfied or pleased by the sacrifice of animals as prescribed under the law; rather by the people learning the prophetic message which those sacrifices were designed to proclaim. For the more learned understood that even God's law was graciously given unto them to show them the things in their lives that had them at odds with God, and to teach them about His very nature.

Psalm 119:26 - I have declared my ways, and You heard me. Teach me Your statutes. 27 Make me to understand the way of Your precepts and so shall I talk of Your wondrous works. 28 My soul melts for heaviness, strengthen me according unto Your word. 29 Remove from me the way of lying and grant me Your law graciously.

Psalm 40:5 - Many, O LORD my God, are Your wonderful works Which You have done; And Your thoughts toward us cannot be recounted to You in order. If I would declare and speak of them, they are more than can be numbered. 6 Sacrifice and offering You did not desire; mine ears have You opened. Burnt offering and sin offering You have not required. 7 Then said I, "Lo, I come, in the volume of the book it is written of Me, 8 I delight to do Your will, O my God, Your law is within my heart."

Hebrews 10:4 - For it is not possible that the blood of bulls and of goats should take away sins. 5 Wherefore when He comes into the world, He said, "Sacrifice and offering You did not desire, but a body You have prepared Me: 6 In burnt offerings and sacrifices for sin You have had no pleasure."

God has always been greatly pleased with those saints who willingly became His servants, even as living sacrifices, holy and acceptable unto Him. This can only be accomplished by our humbling ourselves and embracing the death of the cross and allowing the resurrected life of Christ to live in and through us. This was the key to the sufficiency of God's grace abounding in Paul's life; for the faith of the Son of God in Paul enabled him to be obedient, even to the death of the cross of his own flesh. Now there are many believers who will heatedly argue this doctrinally with you all the day long. Yet regardless of their argument, their lives will always bear witness to the reality of whether they are crucified with Christ or not, and if He is truly living in them.

Matthew 7:18 - A good tree cannot bring forth evil fruit, neither can a corrupt tree bring forth good fruit. 19 Every tree that brings not forth good fruit is hewn down and cast into the fire. 20 Wherefore by their fruits you shall know them. 21 Not everyone that says unto Me,

"Lord, Lord," shall enter into the kingdom of heaven; but he that does the will of My Father which is in heaven.

Galatians 5:24 - And they that are Christ's have crucified the flesh with the affections and lusts. 25 If we [are to] live in the Spirit, [then] let us also walk in the Spirit.

Romans 12:1 - I beseech you therefore, brethren, by the mercies of God, that you would present your bodies a living sacrifice, holy, acceptable unto God, which is your reasonable service. 2 And be not conformed to this world, but be you transformed by the renewing of your mind that you may prove what is that good, and acceptable, and perfect, will of God. 3 For I say, through the grace given unto me, to every man that is among you not to think of himself more highly than he ought to think. But think soberly, according as God has dealt to every man the measure of faith.

Philippians 2:5 - Let this mind be in you, which was also in Christ Jesus: 6 Who, being in the form of God, thought it not robbery to be equal with God: 7 But made Himself of no reputation, and took upon Him the form of a servant and was made in the likeness of men. 8 And being found in fashion as a man, He humbled Himself and became obedient unto death, even the death of the cross.

Don't Run Out of Gas!

I often use the following example when speaking of God's "sufficient" grace. Let's say there is someone who desperately needs to get to another city, but they have no money or means to get there. Nevertheless, they absolutely must get there by a certain time and date, or the consequences will be extreme. Being destitute, they are anxious and don't have any idea what to do. Upon hearing of their plight, I offer them the use of my car to which they say, "Thanks, that would be great, but we still don't have any money for gas." So, I tell them not to worry about it, I will fill up the tank and assure them that there will be more than sufficient gas to get them where they need to go.

Now greatly relieved for having been given all they need to make their journey, they are at peace and confident they will be able to safely complete the trip on time. However, while on their way there they begin thinking about how they have more than enough time to make their trip, and since there is "more than sufficient" gas they decide to take some time to go visit a friend that is just a little bit out of their way. Being caught up in their new found liberty, they soon are driving from one place to another. Eventually they realize the time is getting late, so they begin to head towards their original destination when suddenly to their surprise the car stops abruptly having ran out of gas. If they had only been faithful to use the car and gas for the purpose it was given and not lose sight of where they were supposed to be going.

Hebrews 4:1 - Let us therefore fear, lest, a promise being left us of entering into His rest, any of you should seem to come short of it. 2 For unto us was the gospel preached, as well as unto them: but the word preached did not profit them, not being mixed with faith[*fulness*] in them that heard it.

There was no more reason for these people to run out of gas; no more than there was for God's promise not being realized by the Israelites who died in the wilderness. However, they stubbornly frustrated the sufficient grace of God. But some will argue how they were under the law and we are under grace. But nevertheless, we are serving the very same God under the New Testament and being clearly warned of like consequences; the possibility of coming short of our promised destination if we too decide to disobediently tempt God through either our doubting or rejecting the sufficiency of His grace.

Hebrews 3:7 - Wherefore (as the Holy Ghost says, "Today if you will hear His voice, 8 Harden not your hearts, as in the provocation, in the day of temptation in the wilderness: 9 When your fathers tempted Me, proved Me, and saw My works forty years. 10 Wherefore I was grieved with that generation, and said, 'They do always err in their heart; and they have not known My ways.' 11 So I swore in My wrath, 'They shall not enter into My rest.')" 12 Take heed, brethren, lest there be in any of you an evil heart of unbelief, in departing from the living God. 13 But exhort one another daily while it is called Today; lest any of you be hardened through the deceitfulness of sin. 14 For we are made partakers of Christ if we hold the beginning of our confidence steadfast unto the end.

God gave the Israelites a sure promise; just as sure as all the promises of God made to us in Christ Jesus are Yea, and in Him, Amen. So how could it possibly be that they failed to have God's promise to them be fulfilled?

Numbers 14:34 - After the number of the days in which you searched the land, even forty days, each day for a year, shall you bear your iniquities, even forty years, and you shall know My breach of promise. 35 I the LORD have said, I will surely do it unto all this evil congregation, that are gathered together against me: in this wilderness they shall be consumed, and there they shall die.

What's this? God told them they would know His "breach of promise?" How could this be? Surely God doesn't break His word? There is no doubt that He loved them, and God is no respecter of person, right? And yet what did Peter say when God gave him the revelation of His grace being given unto the Gentiles as well?

Acts 10:34 - Then Peter opened his mouth, and said, "Of a truth I perceive that God is no respecter of persons: 35 But in every nation he that fears Him, and works righteousness, is accepted with Him."

The answer for their failure cannot be attributed to God or His grace: it was simply due to their failure to believe God *and obediently do* what He had told them, to take the promise land by force.

Hebrews 3:19 - So we see that they could not enter in because of unbelief.

Matthew 11:12 - And from the days of John the Baptist until now the kingdom of heaven suffers violence, and the violent take it by force.

Secondly, scriptures clearly state undeniably that God's grace can be frustrated.

Galatians 2:21 - I do not frustrate the grace of God: for if righteousness come by the law, then Christ is dead in vain.

Paul makes it clear that God gave unto him a measure of grace that was sufficient to enable him to both be and do all which God had called him to. This grace wasn't given to Paul because of any sacrificed animal or any other ordinance given under the Levitical priesthood that Paul observed. Rather, the availability of this grace was made possible solely because of what God's wisdom had accomplished through Jesus Christ's death and resurrection.

Christ had freely given Himself so that Paul and people everywhere could be washed and justified of their sins, and thus made suitable to be filled with the Spirit of Christ, men's only hope of glory. It was this indwelling grace of the Spirit of Christ alone that quickened, changed, and enabled Paul to do all that God required of him. Likewise, God desires His grace to so work in all believers, that they too might fulfill that which God requires of everyone who names the name of Christ.

Hebrews 7:11 - If therefore perfection were by the Levitical priesthood, (for under it the people received the law,) what further need was there that another priest should rise after the order of Melchisedec, and not be called after the order of Aaron?

Romans 8:3 - For what the [ceremonial] law could not do in that it was weak through the flesh, God sending His own Son in the likeness of sinful flesh, and for sin, condemned sin in the flesh.

While we are told what the Law could not do in the verse above, it may be beneficial to examine what the Law did do for the children of Israel. For scripture teaches us very clearly that the Law was actually given to the Israelites by God's grace, that they might have a means to recognize the sin in their hearts and have a light for their path in which they could walk with God.

Psalm 119:29 - Remove from me the way of lying: and **grant me Your law graciously**.

Psalm 19:7 - The law of the LORD is perfect, converting the soul: the testimony of the LORD is sure, making wise the simple. 8 The statutes of the LORD are right, rejoicing the heart: the commandment of the LORD is pure, enlightening the eyes. 9 The fear of the LORD is clean, enduring forever: the judgments of the LORD are true and righteous altogether. 10 More to be desired are they than gold, yea than much fine gold: sweeter also than honey and the honeycomb. 11 Moreover by them is Your servant warned: and in keeping of them there is great reward.

Psalm 119:9 - How shall a young man cleanse his way? By taking heed thereto according to Thy word. 10 With my whole heart have I sought You: O let me not wander from Your commandments. 11 Thy word have I hid in mine heart, that I might not sin against You.

Romans 3:1 - What advantage then has the Jew? Or what profit is there of circumcision? 2 Much every way. Chiefly, because unto them were committed the oracles of God.

God's law to the Jews laid the foundation for the revelation of the mystery which was hid from the foundation of the world whereby God was going redeem men from their sin. The Law also clearly summarized righteousness and defined sin even down the minute missing of the mark. For the summary of the Law is clearly to love the Lord God with all our heart, and with all our soul, and with all our strength, and with all our mind, and to love our neighbor as our own selves.

If someone isn't sure how to love God or their neighbor properly, they can study the Ten Commandments which are a thorough summation on how to avoid compromising one's love or breaking commitment to God and man.

For a more in-depth understanding of how the Ten Commandments are to be applied in one's life, they can examine the first five books of the bible in which the basic principles from each commandment are applied to various situations and relationships. These are actual examples of how men heeded the commandments to love God and their neighbor, we have the whole record of scripture whereby we can learn from the successes and failures of others.

Matthew 22:40 - On these two commandments hang all the law and the prophets.

1. You shall love the LORD your God with all your heart, all your soul, and all your might.
   2. You shall love your neighbor as yourself.

NOTE:

For clarity on keeping these two chief commandments please refer to expanded explanations below.

I.   You shall have no other gods before Me.
II. You shall not make any graven images.
III. You shall not take the name of the LORD thy God in vain.
IV. Remember the Sabbath to keep it holy.
V.   Honor your mother and father.
VI. You shall not kill.
VII. You shall not commit adultery.
VIII. You shall not steal.
IX. You shall not lie.
X.   You shall not covet.

Should any further clarification be needed on how to properly love God and your neighbor, please refer to the "Law and Prophets." There you'll find many extensive examples of those who have properly done so, as well as learn of the consequences of those who failed.

Kept under the Law

Perhaps the most common bad rap that is constantly stated by Christians against the Law is when they improperly quote these four words from the following verse, "kept under the law."

Galatians 3:23 - But before faith came, we were kept under the law, shut up unto the faith which should afterwards be revealed.

Many Christians have wrongfully been taught to view this passage as if the phrase "kept under the law" was an oppressive imprisonment; as if they were being taken away, locked up and deprived of their liberty. And while the Greek word which is translated "kept" does in fact mean to be under guard, as if watched by a garrison of soldiers, the implication is not always intended to imply imprisonment; but can often imply protection and preservation as witnessed in the passages below.

Acts 21:31 - And as they went about to kill him, tidings came unto the chief captain of the band, that all Jerusalem was in an uproar. 32 Who immediately took soldiers and centurions and ran down unto them, and when they saw the chief captain and the soldiers, they stopped the beating of Paul.

Act 23:10 - And when there arose a great dissension, the chief captain fearing lest Paul should have been pulled in pieces of them, commanded the soldiers to go down and to take him by force from among them, and to bring him into the castle.

Perhaps even more enlightening is how Peter and Paul both used the same Greek word elsewhere in their epistles.

Philippians 4:7 - And the peace of God, which passes all understanding, shall **keep** your hearts and minds through Christ Jesus.

I Peter 1:5 - Who are **kept** by the power of God through faith unto salvation ready to be revealed in the last time.

Does it sound like God's people were being kept form their liberty in the above verses, or preserved? For the truth is the Israelites were "kept under the law" and their being "shut up unto the faith" simply means the Law was given to prevent the cunning lies of the adversary from gaining access into their hearts and minds. It was God's attempt to insulated them from the damnable heresies of the nations around them with all their devilish idolatries.

The fact is the law was given to Israel to keep their "hearts and minds" from departing from the true and living God and from falling into idolatry and into unbridled immorality. Having been "kept under the Law" was actually a positive thing; for Paul's emphasis was that by the law they were indeed "kept" and were being "shut up [*as in put away for preservation*] unto the faith which should afterwards be revealed."

Sadly, "kept under the Law" is nowadays being presented by many preachers as if God's law had the Israelites pressed down so low that they couldn't hardly move or breathe; as if He was deliberately squashing them. But that is not how Jesus behaved among them, and He was "the brightness of His glory, and the express image of His person," (Hebrews 1:3).

This undue emphasis on their being "under the law" is nothing more than a devilish attempt to misrepresent the Almighty as an angry God who used the law to push men's faces down into the dirt of their sins. Does the following verse from the Old Testament present that oppressive image of God in your hearts when you read it, or one of a merciful and righteous God?

Isaiah 1:18 - Come now, and let us reason together, saith the LORD: though your sins be as scarlet, they shall be as white as snow; though they be red like crimson, they shall be as wool. 19 If you be willing and obedient, you shall eat the good of the land: 20 But if you refuse and rebel, you shall be devoured with the sword for the mouth of the LORD has spoken it.

So, what really was the context in which Paul said "we were kept under the law?"

Galatians 3:21 - Is the law then against the promises of God? God forbid: for if there had been a law given which could have given life, verily righteousness should have been by the law. 22 But the scripture has concluded all under sin that the promise by faith of Jesus Christ might be given to them that believe. 23 But before faith came we were kept under the law, shut up unto the faith which should afterwards be revealed. 24 Wherefore the law was our schoolmaster to bring us unto Christ, that we might be justified by faith. 25 But after that faith is come, we are no longer under a schoolmaster. 26 For you are all the children of God by faith in Christ Jesus.

The Law was never against faith. It is only contrary to faith if one is using it lawlessly; in an attempt to justified themselves when they are actually guilty of transgressing it. Rather the Law, in all its ceremonies and oblations, prophetically foretold the coming of Jesus Christ and His sufferings for sins. However, there was a weakness of the law which was twofold. First, with all the ceremonies, sacrifices, oblations and priestly duties, they were only prophetic actions which pointed to Christ and were not the very object that could redeem men from their sins.

Hebrews 7:18 - For there was a disannulling of the commandment going before for the weakness and unprofitableness thereof. 19 For the law made nothing perfect, but the bringing in of a better hope did; by the which we draw nigh unto God.

Hebrews 10:1 - For the law being a shadow of good things to come and not the very image of the things, could never with those sacrifices which they offered year by year continually make the comers thereunto perfect. 2 For then would they not have ceased to be offered? Because that the worshippers once purged should have had no more conscience of their sins. 3 But in those sacrifices, there was a remembrance again made of sins every year. 4 For it is not possible that the blood of bulls and goats could take away sins. 5 Therefore, when He came into the world, He said, "Sacrifice and offering You did not desire, but a body You have prepared for Me. 6 In burnt offerings and sacrifices for sin You had no pleasure."

Secondly, the law could only reveal to men their sins, but not save men from sin. For there was not an Eleventh Commandment which said "If you have broken any of the first ten, then do this and you shall live." No, the just have always lived by faith, and that my friend is an Old Testament principle that will never change. Men must have faith in the righteousness and mercy of God.

Exodus 34:6 - And the LORD passed by before him, and proclaimed, The LORD, The LORD God, merciful and gracious, longsuffering, and abundant in goodness and truth, 7 Keeping mercy for thousands, forgiving iniquity and transgression and sin, and that will by no means clear the guilty

Habakkuk 2:4 - Behold, his soul which is lifted up is not upright in him: but the just shall live by his faith.

Romans 1:17 - For therein is the righteousness of God revealed from faith to faith: as it is written, "The just shall live by faith."

Romans 8:3 - For what the law could not do, in that it was weak through the flesh, God sending His own Son in the likeness of sinful flesh, and for sin, condemned sin in the flesh: 4 That the righteousness of the law might be fulfilled in us, who walk not after the flesh, but after the Spirit.

It has always been impossible for the law to save men, for as scripture states, it was weak through the flesh; meaning "it is not possible" for dead, unholy men to make themselves holy and alive, or "that the blood of bulls and of goats should take away [their] sins," (Hebrews 10:4).

Therefore, God sent His own Son in the frailty of man's own flesh, yet without sin, to die the death we deserve and by the shedding of His holy blood, through it and it alone, men can now be justified of their sins, fully forgiven and sanctified so as to render them acceptable to receive even the fullness of God's sufficient grace; the indwelling empowerment of the Spirit of Christ living within them.

Galatians 2:20 - I am crucified with Christ: nevertheless, I live; yet not I, but Christ lives in me: and the life which I now live in the flesh I live by the faith of the Son of God, who loved me, and gave Himself for me. 21 I do not frustrate the grace of God: for if righteousness come by the law, then Christ is dead in vain.

I Timothy 1:12 - And I thank Christ Jesus our Lord, who has enabled me, for that He counted me faithful, putting me into the ministry.

Colossians 1:27 - To whom God would make known what is the riches of the glory of this mystery among the Gentiles; which is Christ in you, the hope of glory: 28 Whom we preach, warning every man, and teaching every man in all wisdom; that we may present every man perfect in Christ Jesus: 29 Whereunto I also labor, striving according to His working, which works in me mightily.

And finally, *the third* fundamental truth concerning grace; that God's grace can in fact be received in vain.

> II Corinthians 6:1 - We then, as workers together with Him, beseech you also that you receive not the grace of God in vain.

Yes, it is absolutely true that God's offer of grace to humanity is completely unmerited. For from the beginning, even before the foundations of the world, long before anyone could have even tried to earn, merit, or deserve grace, it was ordained that Jesus Christ would be crucified for our redemption. When sin did abound, grace did abound all the more in that Christ came and willingly died for the ungodly.

But please hear me now, for grace is so, so much more than just "unmerited favor." For God's grace doesn't stop at the forgiveness of our sins; for grace is that indwelling power which quickens dead men and makes them alive and turns sinners into saints. Christ in us is humanity's only hope of glory.

> I Corinthians 1:24 - But unto them which are called, both Jews and Greeks, Christ the power of God, and the wisdom of God.

God's grace is that power alone which delivers us from the sinful nature embedded in our hearts and equips each of us for our unique ministry unto Him and others. So again, it cannot be said enough because it is taught so little; that while grace is indeed unmerited favor, it is much, much more than just unmerited favor. Just as surely as that Word that was with God, was God, for grace is the divine indwelling of the Spirit of Christ the Word. For it is Jesus Himself who empowers us, watches over us, protects us, and guides us as a Shepherd ever towards the victory and makes us overcomers by restoring our souls. It is by this grace and grace alone we are what we are, (or can be as we grow in Christ), or as Paul said, "I am what I am..."

I Corinthians 15:10 - But by the grace of God I am what I am: and His grace which was bestowed upon me was not in vain; but I labored more abundantly than they all: yet not I, but the grace of God which was with me.

Let us never forget that the Kingdom of God suffers violence and our entering in to it will be daily met with the opposition of the adversary. Thus, if we are to take it, we need to put on the whole armor of God and take it just as the Jews did who entered into the Promise Land: for they took it by force. And yet, did not God say He gave it to them? Yes, for it was Him who gave them the victory! Likewise, we need not depend on our own strength, for grace is His power which works in us mightily as we acknowledge His will and exercise our faith in Christ.

Matthew 11:12 - And from the days of John the Baptist until now the kingdom of heaven suffers violence, and the violent take it by force.

Luke 16:16 - The law and the prophets were until John: since that time the kingdom of God is preached and every man presses into it.

The faith that "presses into it" will be a faith that persistently works; for true faith is continually motivated by love.

Galatians 5:6 - For in Jesus Christ neither circumcision avails anything, nor does uncircumcision; but that faith which works by love.

John 14:23 - Jesus answered and said unto him, "If a man loves Me, he will keep My words: and My Father will love him, and We will come unto him, and make Our abode with him. 24 He that loves Me not keeps not My sayings: and the word which you hear is not Mine, but the Father's which sent Me."

Faith works because it is founded upon divine principles. Faith itself is the consequence of truly hearing God's word, which becomes evident when we acknowledge the conviction of the Holy Spirit who bears witness to the truth concerning our sins and God's righteousness and the direction of His will. That consequence of hearing, i.e. our faith, becomes the means or conduit whereby we can receive the promise of grace that enables us to be faithful. For the Apostle Paul said, "For by grace are you saved *through faith*, and that not of yourselves: it is the gift of God."

Let's examine this, because scripture tells us that faith comes by our hearing God's word, and also grace *through that faith* is what saves us. Furthermore, scripture is equally clear that without hearing we could have no faith, as well as it is "through" that faith which comes as a result of our hearing that grace also comes; whereby we are then saved. We must not lose sight of this clear scriptural correlation of *grace through faith*. So, which then is the "gift?" Is it the grace, or is it our faith? What does God's word tell us?

Romans 12:3 - For I say, through the grace given unto me, to every man that is among you not to think of himself more highly than he ought to think. But rather think soberly, according as **God has dealt to every man the measure of faith**.

Every man has been dealt "the measure of faith," but what does that really mean? And what is that measure? It means that God has graciously provided that which is necessary "to every man," an initial measure of faith which is adequate for him to take their first step of faith.

However, this measure of faith will only work in those who humble themselves and acknowledge their personal poverty of spirit, so as to mourn for their sins before a just and holy God. Those who no longer try to excuse themselves or blame someone else or thing for what they are, or for what they have done. For such are those who will truly begin to hunger and thirst for righteousness. It is to such that as these that God will freely give the empowering grace needed for their continued obedience to that faith. Still faith, by its very nature, must continue to increase and be built up, or that grace they have received will have been in vain.

Romans 1:5 - By whom we have received **grace ...for obedience** to the faith among all nations, for His name.

Matthew 5:3 - "Blessed are the poor in spirit, for theirs is the kingdom of heaven. 4 Blessed are those who mourn, for they shall be comforted. 5 Blessed are the meek, for they shall inherit the earth. 6 Blessed are those who hunger and thirst for righteousness, for they shall be filled. 7 Blessed are the merciful, for they shall obtain mercy. 8 Blessed are the pure in heart, for they shall see God. 9 Blessed are the peacemakers, for they shall be called the children of God.

But how can men know these things without hearing the word of God or be able to recognize it as true? It is only by that "measure of faith" which "God has dealt to every man" accompanied by the Spirit of Christ reproving men of their sins.

Be not deceived, every person has been given an adequate measure of faith already given to them. It is there within their conscience via the writing of God's law on their consciences.

Romans 2:14 - For when the Gentiles who do not have the law, by nature still do the things in the law, these although not having the law are a law to themselves. 15 Which shows the work of the law written in their hearts, their conscience also bearing witness, and between themselves their thoughts accusing or else excusing them.

This "measure of faith" which is connected to "the law written in their hearts," is part of the light wherewith Jesus has "lit every man that comes into the world." For without that measure of faith being freely given to all men they would not be able to properly respond to hearing the gospel. Even creation is designed so as to stir up that measure of faith so as to compel all men to seek after God and His truth. So, the only question is will they?

Romans 1:20 - For the invisible things of Him from the creation of the world are clearly seen, being understood by the things that are made, even His eternal power and Godhead; so that they are without excuse.

Consequently, there is no excuse for mankind. Even Wisdom is said to be continually "in the chief place of concourse, in the openings of the gates: in the city she utters her words, saying, "How long you simple ones will you love simplicity? and the scorners delight in their scorning, and fools hate knowledge? Turn you at my reproof and behold, I will pour out My spirit unto you. I will make known My words unto you." Thus, by turning at God's reproof God will give us ears to hear that He might make His word known unto us. Thus, by hearing, we are then given that increase of faith through which His grace can then flood our souls and save us; God pouring out His Spirit unto us and changing us from the inside out, instilling inward virtue to the perfecting of outward godliness.

II Peter 1:5 - And beside this, giving all diligence, add to your faith virtue; and to virtue knowledge; 6 And to knowledge temperance; and to temperance patience; and to patience godliness; 7 And to godliness brotherly kindness; and to brotherly kindness charity. 8 For if these things be in you, and abound, they make you that you shall neither be barren nor unfruitful in the knowledge of our Lord Jesus Christ.

Jesus expects to see these things in us, for by "grace through faith" these things should be in us and abounding. Otherwise we will be proven to have been "barren... [and] unfruitful in the knowledge of our Lord Jesus Christ." Surely none of us would be content or pleased with a friend, or a spouse as our lover, who simply "believes" in us. We would expect and settle for nothing less than faithfulness, and rightly so, because that is the reasonable expectation of a love perfected by grace. True faith will always work towards faithfulness because faith works by love. It really is that simple.

Sadly, many believers continue in sin while rejecting any correction with a rebuttal of "God loves me unconditionally." They have not only minimized God's amazing grace in their hearts to nothing more than "unmerited favor," they have turned it into lasciviousness, which is lawlessness... for they live their lives as it there is no longer a law.

Jude 1:4 - For there are certain men crept in unawares, who were before of old ordained to this condemnation, ungodly men, turning the grace of our God into lasciviousness, and denying the only Lord God, and our Lord Jesus Christ.

Yet Paul clearly stated that when he went unto the Gentiles, he did not go without the law of Christ, for without it he knew the law of the spirit of life in Christ Jesus could not set them free from the law of sin and death.

I Corinthians 9:20 - And unto the Jews I became as a Jew, that I might gain the Jews; to them that are under the [*Mosaic*] law, as under the law, that I might gain them that are under the law; 21 To them that are without law, as without law, (being not without law to God, but under the law to Christ,) that I might gain them that are without law.

Galatians 6:2 - Bear you one another's burdens and so fulfil the law of Christ.

Romans 8:1 - There is therefore now no condemnation to them which are in Christ Jesus, who walk not after the flesh, but after the Spirit. 2 For the law of the Spirit of life in Christ Jesus has made me free from the law of sin and death. 3 For what the law could not do, in that it was weak through the flesh, God sending His own Son in the likeness of sinful flesh, and for sin, condemned sin in the flesh: 4 That the righteousness of the law might be fulfilled in us, who walk not after the flesh, but after the Spirit. 5 For they that are after the flesh do mind the things of the flesh; but they that are after the Spirit the things of the Spirit.

Foolishly, many professing believers live out their lives freely giving way to their flesh and openly continue their friendship with the world. Because they don't really love Him, they don't even try to keep His words beyond mere eye-service before others. Such people have willfully embraced the lie that it really doesn't matter anyway... since God loves them unconditionally and they are saved by His unmerited favor anyway. But is that what Jesus said, or their pastor?

James 4:4 – ...do you not know that the friendship of the world is enmity [*warring with*] with God? Whosoever therefore will be a friend of the world is the enemy of God.

Galatians 5:24 - And they that are Christ's have crucified the flesh with the affections and lusts.

II Thessalonians 2:10 - ...because they received not the love of the truth, that they might be saved. 11 And for this reason God shall send them strong delusion, that they should believe a lie. 12 That they all might be damned who believed not the truth but rather had pleasure in unrighteousness.

John 14:21 – He that has My command-ments and keeps them, he it is that loves Me; and he that loves Me shall be loved of My Father, and I will love him and will manifest Myself to him." 22 Judas said unto Him, not Iscariot, "Lord, how is it that You will manifest Yourself unto us, and not unto the world?" 23 Jesus answered and said unto him, "**IF** a man love Me, he will keep My words: and My Father will love him, and We will come unto him and make Our abode with him. 24 He that loves Me not, keeps not My sayings, and the word which you hear is not Mine, but the Father's which sent Me."

Right there in verse 23 is the biggest word in the bible, and often the most overlooked; "If." For wherever there is an "if" in a passage of scripture, there is always an implied "then." That little two letter word has enormous meaning; for it is always a conditional qualifier that precedes an event or response. "If" is that razor-sharp edge on the sword of the spirit that cuts through all the pretense and good intentions, right to the very heart of every man's faith and proves the integrity of his belief in God. So much so that the beloved Apostle John had this to say.

I John 1:7 - But if we walk in the light, as He is in the light, [*then*] we [*God and us*] have fellowship one with another, and [*then*] the blood of Jesus Christ His Son cleanses us from all sin.

The very first act of grace, *through faith*, is the work of repentance, working faithfulness in us to the commandment of Christ to be holy.

Acts 17:30 - And the times of this ignorance God winked at; but now commands all men everywhere to repent.

Titus 2:11 - For the grace of God that brings salvation has appeared to all men, 12 Teaching us that, denying ungodliness and worldly lusts, we should live soberly, righteously, and godly in this present world.

I Peter 1:13 - Wherefore gird up the loins of your mind, be sober, and hope to the end for the grace that is to be brought unto you at the revelation of Jesus Christ; 14 As obedient children, not fashioning yourselves according to the former lusts in your ignorance: 15 But as He which has called you is holy, so be you holy in all manner of conversation; 16 Because it is written, "Be you holy; for I am holy."

Sadly, many professors of faith today will one day find that they exhausted the grace of God and never even missed it; frustrating it with their stiff-necks and stubborn unfaithfulness. Thus, by neglecting that measure of faith dealt to them, they are the ones who foolishly limited the effectual working of God's grace by burying as it were the proverbial "talent" Christ entrusted them with to invest towards His glory. These are they who will one day find they were actually goats and not the sheep they thought they were when the Lord returns to separate those who profess to know Him.

Psalm 78:41 - Yea, they turned back and tempted God, and limited the Holy One of Israel. 42 They remembered not His hand, nor the day when He delivered them from the enemy [*or their sins*].

Dear reader, this is a very serious matter, because God has given unto us exceeding great and precious promises that enable us to be holy and to live separate from the world's seduction. By His grace, we can be and are to be doers of His word, not hearers only. By His grace we can answer His unique call to each of us and become glorious partakers of His divine nature, having Christ formed in us and thus escape the wrath to come.

I Peter 1:3 - According as His divine power has given unto us all things that pertain unto life and godliness, through the knowledge of Him that has called us to glory and virtue: 4 Whereby are given unto us exceeding great and precious promises: that by these you might be partakers of the divine nature, having escaped the corruption that is in the world through lust.

Some readers, if indeed they have read this far, are already protesting in their minds and arguing how this sounds like salvation by works. But in reality, it is salvation made evident by growth; a witness to true spiritual life, i.e. Christ being formed in us. For this for the perfection of the believer, to the life of Christ in them abounding, which is our only hope of glory. Yet, we only have that life because we humbly received God's word, planting it (as it were) in our hearts.

Romans 5:10 - For if, when we were enemies, we were reconciled to God by the death of His Son, much more, being reconciled, we shall be saved by His life.

James 1:21 - Wherefore lay apart all filthiness and superfluity of naughtiness, and receive with meekness the engrafted word, which is able to save your souls. 22 But be you doers of the word, and not hearers only, deceiving your own selves.

However, though we once received the word, we must also continue in the word, for therein do we abide in Christ, and His life in us, and we grow.

John 15:1 - I am the true vine, and My Father is the husbandman. 2 Every branch in Me that bears not fruit He takes away: and every branch that bears fruit, He purges it, that it may bring forth more fruit. 3 Now you are clean through the word which I have spoken unto you. 4 Abide in Me, and I in you. As the branch cannot bear fruit of itself, except it abide in the vine; no more can you except you abide in Me. 5 I am the vine, you are the branches: He that abides in Me, and I in him, the same brings forth much fruit: for without Me you can do nothing. 6 If a man abides not in Me, he is cast forth as a branch, and is withered; and men gather them, and cast them into the fire and they are burned.

Thus, true salvation will always be evident by growth, which in truth is life. Growth is that proper progress that is expected, just like a seed that germinates and begins to sprout, growing upwards towards the sun. Just like that "engrafted word, which is able to save your souls" that James spoke of, when by faith we allow God's grace to change us, the life in us is just like that seed that sprouted.

Even though a sprout may have just broken through the dirt and pushed out its first two little leaves, it is still perfect. However, it cannot remain that size and be fruitful; it must grow if it is to bring forth fruit. Yet, from germination to harvest, it is nonetheless perfect throughout all the stages of the growing process as long as it is growing; for life is to grow.

I Corinthians 3:5 - Who then is Paul, and who is Apollos, but ministers by whom you have believed, even as the Lord gave to every man? 6 I have planted, Apollos watered; but God gave the increase. 7 So then neither is he that plants anything, neither he that waters; but God that gives the increase.

Ephesians 4:13 - Till we all come in the unity of the faith, and of the knowledge of the Son of God, unto a perfect man, unto the measure of the stature of the fulness of Christ:

14 That we henceforth be no more children, tossed to and fro, and carried about with every wind of doctrine, by the sleight of men, and cunning craftiness, whereby they lie in wait to deceive; 15 But speaking the truth in love, may grow up into Him in all things, which is the head, even Christ: 16 From whom the whole body fitly joined together and compacted by that which every joint supplies, according to the effectual working in the measure of every part, makes increase of the body unto the edifying of itself in love. 17 This I say therefore, and testify in the Lord, that you should no longer walk as other Gentiles walk in the vanity of their mind, 18 Having their understanding darkened, being alienated from the life of God through the ignorance that is in them, because of the blindness of their heart: 19 Who being past feeling have given themselves over unto lasciviousness [*lawlessness*], to work all uncleanness with greediness. 20 But you have not so learned Christ; 21 If so be that you have heard Him and have been taught by Him, as the truth is in Jesus.

II Peter 3:14 - Wherefore, beloved, seeing that you look for such things, be diligent that you may be found of Him in peace, without spot, and blameless. 15 And account that the longsuffering of our Lord is salvation; even as our beloved brother Paul also according to the wisdom given unto him has written unto you; 16 As also in all his epistles, speaking in them of these things; in which are some things hard to be understood which they that are unlearned and unstable wrestle with, as they do also the other scriptures unto their own destruction. 17 You therefore, beloved, seeing that you know these things before, beware lest you also are led away with the error of the wicked and fall from your own steadfastness. 18 But grow in grace and in the knowledge of our Lord and Savior Jesus Christ. To Him be glory both now and forever. Amen.

No Excuse

Even though Adam sinned and caused all humanity to inherit his fallen nature and needing to escape the corruption that is in the world through lust; the mystery of godliness which was hid from the foundation of the world has left no excuse for any to continue in their sin. For God foresaw sin with all its corruption and consequences, even before anything was created. His remedy was always there available through faith, and in the fulness of time was fully revealed in the Gospel of Jesus Christ.

Therefore, it must be recognized as an indisputable fact that God foresaw absolutely everything, in infinitesimal detail, and categorically knew every good and evil thing that would transpire throughout all eternity. Therefore, before the creation of man, God fully knew all the circumstances which would occur and every force of evil that would arise in opposition to us with all its intensity, intended destruction, and plans of confusion.

Accordingly, God has made all the necessary preparations to assure His own purposes and glory. That regardless of the foe or their evil intent, He can absolutely assure those who love Him that each and every circumstance and event in their lives was foreseen and therefore He can successfully work all things together for their eternal well-being.

The foreknowledge of sin erupting in His creation didn't discourage God. Rather, He willingly created humanity in His image, knowing that as lights they could still brilliantly manifest the wonders and glory of God through the sufficiency of His amazing grace which is made available to all through Jesus Christ the Lord.

Each of us were created to be temples for the Spirit of the living God and are called to "serve the LORD with gladness… [*for*] the LORD He is God: it is He that has made us, and not we ourselves; we are His people, and the sheep of His pasture."

Every person who has ever lived has been "His workmanship, created in Christ Jesus unto good works, which God has before ordained that we should walk in them." So then, what will sinners say in their defense when they are asked by their Creator why they continually ignored His calling out to them?

Consequently, it is irrelevant how people choose to view and dismiss their sin. For what God sees in sin is the willingness of men to trample His Son in order to continue down their own path with a callous indifference for Jesus' precious blood. Sadly, many of those who profess His name have in their hearts devalued His precious blood to the status of a common product readily available on the shelves of the local convenient stores. They assume His blood will always be there whenever they need it and decide to repent, or just ask for forgiveness.

Such people are actually sitting in churches on Sunday feeling all justified while continuing in their idolatry by worshipping "another Jesus" made by the modern commercial church system just for them so they continue to come and support a dead hypocritical religious system.

II Corinthians 11:4 - If indeed someone is coming to preach another Jesus, whom I did not preach, or you are receiving a Spirit other than you once received, or another gospel which you did not accept before, you would do well to bear with me. *(Montgomery's New Testament)*

Matthew 23:13 - "But woe to you, scribes and Pharisees, hypocrites! For you shut up the kingdom of heaven against men. For you neither go in yourselves, nor do you allow those who are entering to go in. 14 Woe to you, scribes and Pharisees, hypocrites! For you devour widows' houses, and for a pretense make long prayers. Therefore, you will receive greater condemnation. 15 "Woe to you, scribes and Pharisees, hypocrites! For you travel land and sea to win one proselyte, and when he is won, you make him twice as much a son of hell as yourselves.

Dear reader, if Jesus so warned us that "Many will say to Me in that day, Lord, Lord, have we not prophesied in Your name? And in Your name have cast out devils? And in Your name done many wonderful works?" Don't you think it is best you are sure you know who He was talking about and why? Otherwise He might end up saying to you as well, "I never knew you. Depart from Me you who work iniquity."

Please, don't let that happen. Jesus Christ is worthy of all your love, your adoration, praise and worship. Seek the Lord while He may be found.

Romans 12:1 - I beseech you therefore, brothers, by the mercies of God to present your bodies a living sacrifice, holy, pleasing to God, which is your reasonable service. 2 And do not be conformed to this world, but be transformed by the renewing of your mind, in order to prove by you what is that good and pleasing and perfect will of God.

Awake!

Awake, you sleeper! Awake! Arise and make yourself ready! It's time to put aside those childish pursuits and your endless musing with vanities. Awake, I say! Do you not realize the time in which you are privileged to live? Now more than ever can the sound of the bridegroom's coming be heard. Surely, He is drawing near.

The need to purify yourself has grown greater, for the time allotted has grown shorter. The dark of night has already conquered the eastern horizon as the sun glow fades in the west. The King had long ago sent out His invitation. He proclaimed to all, "COME!"

Yes, come, and do make haste! Do you not know that if you refuse to comply with the King that His anger will be kindled against you? Yet in His patience and longsuffering He still says, "Come! Come to the greatest of all feasts! There is food, wine, and much song and dance. Joyful dance to celebrate the wedding of all weddings. Come and attend My wedding, come and be part of My bride."

The Bridegroom has long been ready, yet He has patiently waited. He has waited for you! Arise therefore you sleeper! So much remains for you to do. TODAY you must prepare. Set aside your complacency and strive to mature!

Strive to increase your knowledge and grow in your understanding so you might be completely resolved to live your life solely for the King of kings! Rise up and cast out reservation and hesitation, these are foes that have hindered and killed countless before you.

Arise! Answer His call!

It is your only reasonable response . . .

"Awake you who sleep, and arise from the dead, for Christ shall give you light.

Awake to righteousness and sin not. For some *[of you]* have not the *[intimate]* knowledge of God. I speak this to your shame."

(Eph. 6:14, I Cor. 15:34)

Made in the USA
Columbia, SC
20 April 2023

15616020R00100